THE JESUS LIBRARY

THE HARD SAYINGS OF JESUS

THE JESUS LIBRARY

edited by Michael Green

THE HARD SAYINGS OF JESUS

F. F. Bruce
Emeritus Professor
University of Manchester

HODDER AND STOUGHTON
LONDON SYDNEY AUCKLAND TORONTO

British Library Cataloguing in Publication Data

Bruce, F. F.
   The hard sayings of Jesus.—(The Jesus library)—
   (Hodder Christian paperbacks)
   1. Jesus Christ—Teachings
   I. Title   II. Series
   232.9′54   BS2415

IBSN 0 340 27044 6

Hodder and Stoughton Editorial Office: 47 Bedford Square, London WC1B 3DP

To my students
in the University of Manchester
1959–1978

ABBREVIATIONS

AV	Authorised (King James) Version of the English Bible
L	Material peculiar to the Gospel of Luke
M	Material peculiar to the Gospel of Matthew
NEB	New English Bible
NIV	New International Version
Q	Material common to the Gospels of Matthew and Luke but not found in the Gospel of Mark
RSV	Revised Standard Version (1946–1952)
RV	Revised Version (1881–1885)

CONTENTS

INTRODUCTION

Many of those who listened to Jesus during his public ministry found some of his sayings 'hard', and said so. Many of those who read his sayings today, or hear them read in church, also find them hard, but do not always think it fitting to say so.

Our Lord's sayings were all of a piece with his actions and with his way of life in general. The fewer preconceptions we bring from outside to the reading of the Gospels, the more clearly shall we see him as he really was. It is all too easy to believe in a Jesus who is largely a construction of our own imagination – an inoffensive person whom no one would really trouble to crucify. But the Jesus whom we meet in the Gospels, far from being an inoffensive person, gave offence right and left. Even his loyal followers found him, at times, thoroughly disconcerting. He upset all established notions of religious propriety. He spoke of God in terms of intimacy which sounded like blasphemy. He seemed to enjoy the most questionable company. He set out with open eyes on a road which, in the view of 'sensible' people, was bound to lead to disaster.

But in those who were not put off by him he created a passionate love and allegiance which death could not destroy. They knew that in him they had found the way of acceptance, peace of conscience, life that was life indeed. More than that: in him they came to know God himself in a new way; here was the life of God being lived out in a real human life, and communicating itself through him to them. And there are many people today who meet Jesus, not in Galilee and Judaea but in the gospel record, and become similarly aware of his powerful attractiveness, entering into the same experience as those who made a positive response to him when he was on earth.

One reason for the complaint that Jesus's sayings were hard was that he made his hearers think. For some people thinking is a difficult and uncomfortable exercise, especially when it involves the critical reappraisal of firmly held prejudices and convictions, or the challenging of the current consensus of opinion. Any utterance, therefore, which invites them to engage in this kind of thinking is a hard saying. Many of Jesus's sayings were hard in this sense. They suggested that it would be good to reconsider things that every reasonable person accepted. In a world where the race was to the swift and the battle to the strong, where the prizes of life went to the pushers and the go-getters, it was preposterous to congratulate the unassertive types and tell them that *they* would inherit the earth or, better still, possess the kingdom of heaven. Perhaps the beatitudes were, and are, the hardest of Jesus's sayings.

For the Western world today the hardness of many of Jesus's sayings is all the greater because we live in a different culture from that in which they were uttered, and speak a different language from his. He appears to have spoken Aramaic for the most part, but with few exceptions his Aramaic words have not been preserved. His words have come down to us in a translation, and that translation – the Greek of the Gospels – has to be retranslated into our own language. But when the linguistic problems have been resolved as far as possible and we are confronted by his words in what is called a 'dynamically equivalent' version – that is, a version which aims at producing the same effect in us as the original words produced in their first hearers – the removal of one sort of difficulty may result in the raising of another.

For to us there are two kinds of hard saying: there are some which are hard to understand and there are some which are only too easy to understand. When sayings of Jesus which are hard in the former sense are explained in dynamically equivalent terms, then they are likely to become hard in the latter sense. Mark Twain spoke for many when he said that the things in the Bible that bothered him were not those that he did not understand but those that he did understand. This is particularly true of the sayings of Jesus. The better we understand them, the harder they are to take. (Perhaps, similarly, this is why some religious people show such hostility to modern versions of the Bible: these versions make the meaning plain, and the plain meaning is unacceptable.)

If the following pages explain the hard sayings of Jesus in such a way as to make them more acceptable, less challenging, then the probability is that the explanation is wrong. Jesus did not go about mouthing pious platitudes; had he done so, he would not have made as many enemies as he did. 'The common people heard him gladly', we are told – more gladly, at any rate, than members of the religious establishment did – but even among the common people many were disillusioned when he turned out not to be the kind of leader they hoped he would be.

Apart from the one archetypal hard saying with which our collection starts, all the sayings treated here come from the synoptic Gospels. The Gospel of John has hard sayings in plenty, but they have a character of their own, and to deal with them would call for another volume of the same dimensions as this.

The view of the interrelatedness of the synoptic Gospels taken in this work does not greatly affect the exposition of the hard sayings, but it will be as well to state briefly here what that view is. It is that the Gospel of Mark provided Matthew and Luke with one of their major sources; that Matthew and Luke shared another common source, an arrangement of sayings of Jesus set in a brief narrative framework (not unlike the arrangement of the prophetic books of the Old Testament); and that each of the synoptic evangelists had access also to sources of information not used by the others.[1] It helps at times to see how one evangelist understood his predecessor by recasting or amplifying his wording.

Some of the sayings appear in different contexts in different Gospels. On this it is often said that Jesus must not be thought incapable of repeating himself. This is freely conceded: he may well have used a pithy saying on a variety of occasions. There is no reason to suppose that he said 'He who has ears to hear, let him hear', or 'Many are called, but few are chosen', once only. But there are occasions when a saying, indicated by comparative study to have been spoken in one particular set of circumstances, is assigned to different contexts by different evangelists or different sources. There are other principles of arrangement than the purely chronological: one writer may group a number of sayings together because they deal with the same subject-matter or have the same literary form; another, because they have a common keyword (like the sayings about fire and salt in Mark 9:43–50).

Where there is reason to think that an evangelist has placed a saying in a topical rather than a chronological setting, it can be interesting to try to decide what its chronological setting in the ministry of Jesus probably was. For example, it has been suggested that the saying 'You are Peter', which Matthew (alone of the synoptic evangelists) includes in the report of Jesus's interchange with the disciples at Caesarea Philippi (see p. 139), may have belonged chronologically to another occasion, such as Jesus's appearance to Peter in resurrection. Even more speculative is the interpretation of some of the sayings as words of Jesus spoken not during his public ministry but later, through the mouth of a prophet in the early church. It has been thought best in this work not to engage in such speculation but to treat the sayings primarily in the contexts provided for them by the evangelists.

Again, this does not seem to be the place for an enquiry into the question whether the sayings examined are authentic sayings of Jesus or not. To help students in answering such a question some scholars have formulated 'criteria of authenticity' for application to the sayings recorded in the Gospels. One scholar, who attached great importance to these criteria, told me a few years ago that he had concluded that among all the sayings ascribed to Jesus in the Gospels, only six, or at most eight, could be accepted as undoubtedly his. The reader of this work will realise that it is written from a less sceptical viewpoint than that. Let this be said, however: the fact that a saying is hard is no ground for suspecting that Jesus did not say it. On the contrary, the harder it is, the more likely it is to be genuine.

The second volume of the *Encyclopaedia Biblica*, published

in 1901, contained a long and important entry on 'Gospels' by a Swiss scholar, P. W. Schmiedel. In the course of this he listed a number of sayings of Jesus and other passages which, to his mind, ran so much counter to the conception of Jesus which quickly became conventional in the Church that no one could be thought to have invented them. He therefore regarded their authenticity as beyond dispute and proposed to treat them as 'the foundation-pillars for a truly scientific life of Jesus'. Several of them will come up for inspection in the following pages for, whether in Schmiedel's sense or otherwise, they are certainly hard sayings.

The biblical version most frequently quoted in this work is the Revised Standard Version. It is for the most part in the wording of the Authorised (King James) Version that the sayings studied have acquired the status of 'hard sayings', and the RSV wording is sufficiently close to that of the AV to retain the same element of 'hardness'. A version like the New English Bible sometimes removes one hardness to replace it by another.

In the interpretation of the sayings quoted I am, of course, indebted to many other interpreters. Some acknowledgment of my indebtedness is made in the following pages. There is one interpreter, however, to whom I am conscious of a special debt: that is the late Professor T. W. Manson, particularly in respect of his two works *The Teaching of Jesus*[2] and *The Sayings of Jesus*.[3] From the latter of these works I take leave to borrow words which will supply a fitting conclusion to this introduction:

It will simplify the discussion if we admit the truth at the outset: that the teaching of Jesus is difficult and unacceptable because it runs counter to those elements in human nature which the twentieth century has in common with the first – such things as laziness, greed, the love of pleasure, the instinct to hit back and the like. The teaching as a whole shows that Jesus was well aware of this and recognised that here and nowhere else lay the obstacle that had to be surmounted.[4]

1.

EATING THE FLESH AND DRINKING THE BLOOD OF THE SON OF MAN

'Truly, truly, I say to you, unless you eat the flesh of the Son of man and drink his blood, you have no life in you' (John 6:53)

This was the original hard saying: as John reports, 'many of his disciples, when they heard it, said, "This is a hard saying; who can listen to it?"' (John 6:60). The implication is that they not only found it difficult to understand, but suspected that, if they did understand it, they would find it unacceptable. The NEB expresses a different nuance by its rendering: 'This is more than we can stomach! Why listen to such talk?' That implies that they thought Jesus was talking nonsense, and that it was a waste of time listening to it; but that is probably not what John means.

The feeding of the five thousand is one of the few incidents in the ministry of Jesus recorded by all four evangelists. The narrative of Mark 6:31–52 (including the sequel in which Jesus came walking to his disciples across the water) is reproduced substantially in Matthew 14:13–33 and (without the walking on the water) in Luke 9:10–17. John tells the story independently (together with the walking on the water) in John 6:1–21.

In the synoptic Gospels we get the impression that there was more in the feeding of the multitude than met the eye at the time or meets the reader's eye today. Mark in particular makes it plain that the feeding was intended to teach the disciples a lesson which they failed to learn, and that Jesus was surprised at their failure. When Jesus had joined them in the boat on their way back to the other side of the lake of Galilee, and the strong head wind which had made progress so difficult for them stopped blowing, then, says Mark, 'they were utterly astounded, for they did not understand about the loaves, but their hearts were hardened' (Mark 6:51–52). 'Their hearts were hardened' means 'their minds were closed', as the NEB puts it: they were too obtuse to take the lesson in, and the lesson evidently had something to do with the person of their Master.

But the further meaning which lies beneath the surface of the synoptic record is brought up above the surface by John and spelt out in detail. He does this in the form of an address given by Jesus shortly afterwards in the synagogue at Capernaum. The subject of the discourse is the bread of life. It has been suggested that on that sabbath day one of the scripture lessons in the synagogue was Exodus 16:13–36 or Numbers 11:4–9, which tell of the manna, the bread from heaven with which the Israelites were fed during their wilderness wanderings. At any rate, this is the subject with which the address begins.

The manna which their ancestors ate in the wilderness, Jesus tells his hearers, was not the food of immortality: those who ate it died nevertheless – some sooner, some later. Similarly, the bread with which he had recently fed the multitude was but material bread. They wished to make him their leader because he had given them that bread, but really he had come to give them better bread than that. Just as he had offered the Samaritan woman at Jacob's well better water than that in the well, the eternally satisfying water of life, so now he offers these Galileans better bread than the loaves with which the five thousand had been fed, better bread even than the manna which their forefathers had eaten, 'the food which endures to eternal life'. The manna might be called bread from heaven, even the bread of God; but the true 'bread of God is that which comes down from heaven, and gives life to the world' (John 6:27–34). Not only so, but God has one authorised and certified agent to bestow this life-giving bread: that is the Son of man,

Jesus himself. So far, so good: as the Samaritan woman, hearing of the water of life, said, 'Sir, give me this water, that I may not thirst' (John 4:15), so now Jesus's present hearers say, 'Sir, give us this bread always.'

This sets the stage for the next step of the lesson. Jesus not only *gives* the bread of life; he *is* the bread of life. True life, eternal life, is to be had in him alone: 'he who comes to me shall not hunger, and he who believes in me shall never thirst' (John 6:35). Indeed, not only will those who come to him in faith find in him perpetual sustenance and refreshment for their souls' hunger and thirst; they will never die. 'I am the living bread which came down from heaven; any one who eats of this bread will live for ever; and the bread which I shall give for the life of the world is my flesh' (John 6:51).

Now the lesson really begins to be hard. Anyone who has the advantage of reading these words in the context of the whole Gospel of John knows what their purport is. To believe in Christ is not only to give credence to what he says: it is to be united to him by faith, to participate in his life. Up to a point, his words about giving his flesh for the life of the world are paralleled in Mark 10:45, where he speaks of the Son of man as coming 'to give his life a ransom for many'. In the language which Jesus spoke 'my flesh' could be another way of saying 'myself': he himself is the bread given for the life of the world. But the saying in Mark 10:45 makes no reference to the Son of man as food for the souls of the 'many'; this is an additional emphasis, and one which leaves the synagogue congregation out of its depth.

On the lips of people who felt out of their depth, the question 'How can this man give us his flesh to eat?' (John 6:52) was a natural one. But it is John's practice when recording Jesus's discourses or conversations to quote words which have a spiritual meaning and then make the hearers show by their response that they have failed to grasp that meaning; Jesus is thus given an opportunity to repeat his words more fully. So here he repeats himself more fully in reply to the congregation's bewilderment: 'he who eats my flesh and drinks my blood has eternal life, and I will raise him up at the last day. For my flesh is food indeed, and my blood is drink indeed. He who eats my flesh and drinks my blood abides in me, and I in him' (John 6:54–56).

What could he mean? Plainly his language was not to be taken literally: he was not advocating cannibalism. But how was it to be taken? It was not only obscure, they thought: it was offensive. For Jews the drinking of any blood, even the eating of flesh from which the blood had not been completely drained, was taboo. But drinking the blood of a human being was an idea which ought not even to be mentioned. This was a hard saying in more senses than one.

Jesus answered their protest by pointing out that his words were to be understood spiritually. 'It is the spirit that gives life, the flesh is of no avail' (John 6:63). The physical or literal meaning of the words was plainly ruled out. But what was the spiritual meaning?

Again the reader of this Gospel, viewing these words in the context of the whole work, has an advantage over the first hearers, who had no such explanatory context. What we have in Jesus's strange language is a powerful metaphor stating that a share in the life of God, eternal life, is granted to those who in faith come to Jesus, appropriate him, enter into union with him. On this let two doctors of the Church be heard: Augustine of Hippo (at the end of the fourth century) and Bernard of Clairvaux (twelfth century).

The hard saying cannot be taken literally, says Augustine, since it would seem to be enjoining a crime or a vice: 'it is therefore a figure, bidding us communicate in the sufferings of our Lord, and secretly and profitably treasure in our hearts the fact that his flesh was crucified and pierced for us.'[1] Elsewhere he sums the matter up in an epigram: *Crede et manducasti*, 'Believe, and thou hast eaten.'[2]

Bernard expounds the words 'he who eats my flesh and drinks my blood has eternal life' as meaning: 'He who reflects on my death, and after my example mortifies his members which are on earth, has eternal life – in other words, "If you suffer with me, you will also reign with me."'[3]

The question is naturally raised: What relation do these

words of Jesus bear to the communion service, in which believers receive bread and wine as tokens of the body and blood of the Lord? Since John, unlike the other evangelists, does not record the institution of the Holy Communion, it could be said that this discourse represents his counterpart to their accounts of what Jesus did and said in the upper room when he gave his disciples the bread and the cup (see pp. 236-9). In the discourse of John 6 Jesus is not making a direct reference to the Holy Communion, but this discourse conveys the same truth in words as the Holy Communion conveys in action. This truth is summed up in the invitation extended to the communicant in the *Book of Common Prayer*: 'Take and eat this in remembrance that Christ died for thee, and feed on him in thy heart by faith with thanksgiving.' To feed on Christ in one's heart by faith with thanksgiving is to 'eat the flesh of the Son of man and drink his blood' and so have eternal life. (On the phrase 'the Son of man' see pp. 27, 246.)

2.

THE SON OF MAN FORGIVING SINS

'The Son of man has authority on earth to forgive sins'
(Mark 2:10)

When the four friends of the paralysed man broke through the roof of the house in Capernaum where Jesus was teaching, and lowered him on his pallet at Jesus's feet, Jesus appreciated their faith and determination and healed the man. But before he told the man to pick up his pallet and walk out with it, he said to him, 'My son, your sins are forgiven' (Mark 2:5). Nothing is said of the cause of the man's paralysis, but Jesus evidently recognised that the first thing he needed was the assurance that his sins were forgiven. If this assurance were accepted, the physical cure would follow.

His words to the paralysed man constituted a hard saying in the ears of some of the bystanders. Who was this to pronounce forgiveness of sins? To forgive injuries that one has received oneself is a religious duty, but sins are committed against God, and therefore God alone may forgive them. One may say to a sinner, 'May God forgive you'; but by what authority can one say to him, 'Your sins are forgiven'? Probably Jesus's critics would have agreed that a duly authorised spokesman of God might, in the words of the General Absolution, 'declare and pronounce to his people, being penitent, the absolution and remission of their sins'; but they did not acknowledge Jesus as such a duly authorised spokesman, nor was there any evidence, so far as they could see, that repentance was forthcoming or that an appropriate sin-offering had been presented to God. It was the note of authority in Jesus's voice as he pronounced forgiveness that gave chief offence to them: he imposed no conditions, called for no amendment of life, but spoke as though his bare word ensured the divine pardon. He was really arrogating to himself the prerogative of God, they thought.

How could Jesus give evidence of his authority to forgive sins? They could not see sins being forgiven, but they could see the effect of Jesus's further words in the man's response. It is easy to *say* 'Your sins are forgiven', because no one can ordinarily see whether sins are forgiven or not. But if one tells a paralysed man to get up and walk, the words will quickly be shown to be empty words if nothing happens. 'So,' said Jesus to his critics, 'that you may know that the Son of man has authority on earth to forgive sins,' and then, addressing himself to the paralytic, 'rise, take up your pallet, and go home.' When the paralytic did just that, Jesus's power as a healer was confirmed – but more than that, it was the assurance that his sins were forgiven that enabled the man to do what a moment previously would have been impossible, so Jesus's authority to forgive sins was confirmed at the same time.

This is the first occurrence of the designation 'the Son of man' in Mark's Gospel, and one of the two occurrences in his Gospel to be located before Peter confessed Jesus to be the Christ at Caesarea Philippi (the other being the statement in Mark 2:28 that the Son of man is lord of the sabbath; see p. 34). 'The Son of man' was apparently Jesus's favourite way of referring to himself (see pp. 34, 154). Sometimes the 'one like a son of man' who receives supreme authority in Daniel's vision of the day of judgment (Dan. 7:13–14) may provide the background to Jesus's use of the expression (see p. 246), but that son of man is authorised to execute judgment rather than to pronounce forgiveness (one may compare John 5:27, where the Father has given the Son 'authority to execute judgment, because he is son of man'). Here, however, the expression more probably points to Jesus as the representative man – 'the Proper Man, whom God himself hath bidden'. This is how Matthew appears to have understood it: he concludes his account of the incident by saying that the crowds that saw it 'glorified God, who had given such authority to men' – that is, to human beings (Matt. 9:8). The authority so given is exercised by Jesus as the representative man – or, as Paul was later to put it, the 'last Adam' (1 Cor. 15:45). To pronounce, and bestow, forgiveness of sins is the highest prerogative of God, and this he has shared with the Son of man.

3.

NOT THE RIGHTEOUS BUT SINNERS

'I came not to call the righteous, but sinners' (Mark 2:17)

Nineteen centuries and more of gospel preaching and New Testament reading have familiarised us with the idea that Jesus's ministry was specially directed to sinners – not simply to sinners in the sense in which most people will admit that 'we are all sinners', but sinners in the sense that their lives offended the accepted moral code of their community. 'The saying is sure and worthy of full acceptance, that Christ Jesus came into the world to save sinners' (1 Tim. 1:15); this is a great gospel text, and if the writer goes on to speak of himself as first and foremost among sinners, that serves to underline his claim on the saving grace of Christ. But during the ministry of Jesus it gave great offence to many respectable people that a religious teacher as he was should have so little regard for what was expected of him as to consort with those who were no better than they should be. 'If this man were a prophet,' said Simon the Pharisee to himself, when Jesus allowed a woman of doubtful reputation to touch him, 'he would have known ... what sort of woman this is who is touching him, for she is a sinner' (Luke 7:39). But Jesus knew perfectly well what sort of woman she was, and for that very reason would not prevent her from paying him such embarrassing attention (see p. 80).

Among all the traditional designations of Jesus, probably none is more heart-warming than 'the friend of sinners'. But this designation was first given to him by way of criticism: 'a glutton and a drunkard,' they said, 'a friend of tax collectors and sinners!' (Luke 7:34) – tax-collectors occupying the lowest rung on the ladder of respectability, matched only by harlots. It was not that he tolerated such people, as though he did them a favour by taking notice of them, *de haut en bas*: he gave the impression that he liked their company, that he even preferred it; he did not condemn them but encouraged them to feel at home with him. 'This man receives sinners', the scribes said by way of complaint; and more than that, he actually 'eats with them' (Luke 15:2). To accept invitations to a meal in the homes of such people, to enjoy table-fellowship with them – that was the most emphatic way of declaring his unity with them. No wonder this gave offence to those who, sometimes with considerable painstaking, had kept to the path of sound morality. If a man is known by the company he keeps, Jesus was simply asking to be known as the friend of the ne'er-do-wells, the dregs of society. And would not many religious people today react in exactly the same way?

On one occasion when Jesus had accepted a dinner invitation in the home of one of these disreputable people, his disciples were approached by the scribes. The disciples were included in the invitation, but some of them may have had misgivings. 'Why does he eat with tax collectors and sinners?' they were asked. But Jesus interposed with the answer. 'It is sick people, not healthy people, who need the doctor,' he said; 'it is sinners, not righteous people, that I came to call' (Mark 2:17). To call means to invite: he had accepted their invitation, but they received an invitation from him – to take and enjoy the loving mercy of the heavenly Father. It is inevitable that the 'ninety-nine righteous persons who need no repentance' (Luke 15:7) should feel that too much fuss is made over sinners (see p. 170), but since the gospel is for sinners first and foremost – indeed, for sinners only – it cannot be otherwise.

These words of Jesus are reproduced by the two other synoptic evangelists (Matt. 9:13; Luke 5:32), but Luke adds a short explanatory gloss: 'I have not come to call the righteous, but sinners *to repentance*.' Repentance figures more frequently in Luke's Gospel than in the other two (it does not figure at all in the Gospel of John). It has sometimes been suggested that Luke's addition betrays a misunderstanding on his part, but this is not really so. If repentance in the teaching of Jesus implies change of character rather than reformation of behaviour,[1] then Jesus believed in dealing with the root of the disease and not merely with the symptoms. And the root could be dealt with effectively only by the practical assurance and demonstration of outgoing, self-giving love.

4.

THE SABBATH FOR MAN

'The sabbath was made for man, not man for the sabbath; so the Son of man is lord even of the sabbath' (Mark 2:27–28)

This is the second occurrence of the designation 'the Son of man' in Mark's Gospel – one of the two occurrences which he places before the Caesarea Philippi incident. (For the first see p. 26.) The words were the conclusion of Jesus's reply to those who criticised his disciples for plucking ears of grain as they walked through the fields one sabbath and then (according to Luke 6:1) eating the grain when they had rubbed the ears in their hands to separate the kernel from the husk. Harmless enough actions, it might be supposed today (unless the owner of the crop complained that he was being robbed), but plucking the ears was technically regarded by the interpreters of the law as a form of reaping, and rubbing them to extract the kernel as a form of grinding, and reaping and grinding were two kinds of work that were forbidden on the sabbath. Probably, in addition to the expressed criticism of the disciples, there was an implied criticism of Jesus for allowing them to break the law in this way.

Jesus first invoked a precedent: in an emergency David had been permitted by the priest in charge of the sanctuary at Nob (perhaps on Mount Scopus, near Jerusalem) to have some of the holy bread (the 'shewbread' or 'bread of the [divine] presence') for himself and his followers to eat, although it was laid down in the law that none but priests should eat it (1 Sam.

21:1–6). The point of Jesus's argument here seems to be that human need takes priority over ceremonial law; it is relevant to recall that in traditional interpretation (though not in the Old Testament text) the incident from the life of David took place on a sabbath (the day when, according to Leviticus 24:8–9, the old bread was to be removed, to be eaten by 'Aaron and his sons ... in a holy place', and replaced by new bread, 'set in order before the Lord').

But Jesus went on to invoke an earlier and higher precedent (see p. 45). The sabbath was instituted by God; what was God's purpose in instituting it? If that can be discovered, then the sabbath law is best kept when God's purpose in giving it is best fulfilled. In Genesis 2:2–3, God is said to have 'rested' on the seventh day when he had finished the creative work of the six preceding days, so he 'blessed the seventh day and hallowed it'. The Hebrew verb translated 'rest' is *shābath*, which is given here as the explanation of the word 'sabbath' (Hebrew *shabbāth*). Neither Jesus nor his critics thought that God needed to rest on the seventh day because he was tired after a hard week's work. He 'ceased' or 'desisted' from his work. Why, then, did he 'bless' the sabbath day and 'hallow' it? Not for his own sake, but for the sake of his creatures who, he knew, would certainly need to rest after a hard week's work. This is implied in the Genesis narrative itself. The fourth commandment, in the form which it is given in Exodus 20: 8–11, bids the Israelites sanctify the seventh day by refraining from work, because God sanctified it by ceasing from his work after the six days of creation. But in the form which this commandment is given in Deuteronomy 5:12–15 it is made explicitly clear that the sabbath was given for the sake of those who need to rest after hard work: 'that your manservant and your maidservant may rest as well as you'.

The sabbath day was instituted, then, to meet a human need, and the day is best sanctified when human need is met on it. Expositors regularly quote as a parallel the words of Rabbi Simeon ben Menasya preserved in a rabbinical commentary on Exodus 31:14: 'The sabbath is delivered to you; you are not delivered to the sabbath.'[1]

But the real problem of Jesus's saying is the significance of the 'so' or 'so that' introducing the next words: 'the Son of man is lord even of the sabbath'. How does it follow from the fact that the sabbath was made for man that the Son of man is lord of the sabbath? In one way, this would not have been so much of a problem for those who first heard Jesus speak the words. Since 'man' was regularly expressed in Aramaic by the idiom 'son of man', the literal translation of the saying would have been: 'The sabbath was made for the son of man, not the son of man for the sabbath; so the son of man is lord even of the sabbath.' The question that would rise in the hearers' minds was: 'In what sense is the son of man lord of the sabbath? Does he mean that humanity in general is lord of the sabbath?' This question confronts us too, but we have a further question to think about: why did Mark use the simple noun 'man' (human being, or the human race) in the first two clauses, but the locution 'the Son of man' in the third? He must have intended the subject of the third clause to mean something more than man in general. If so, what was that something more? Jesus probably meant that he who is lord of the sabbath, he who has the sovereign authority to interpret the sabbath law in accordance with the divine purpose in instituting it, is the representative man, and that is the role which he now discharges. Since the sabbath was made for man, he whom God has ordained to be man's representative before him is authorised to dispose of the sabbath at his own discretion.

5.

NOT DEAD BUT SLEEPING

'Why do you make a tumult and weep? The child is not dead but sleeping' (Mark 5:39)

The statement that Jairus's twelve-year-old daughter was 'not dead, but sleeping' appears in all three synoptic narratives (cf. Matt. 9:24; Luke 8:52). But what did Jesus mean when he said so? The girl's death had certainly been reported: as Jesus was on the way to the house where she lived, in response to her father's anguished plea to him to come and lay his healing hands on her, a messenger came to say that she had died; therefore, 'why trouble the Teacher any further?' But Jesus encouraged her father: 'Do not be afraid; only believe', and went on with him to the house. It was then that he rebuked the crowd that had gathered for the noise they were making. Did he mean that she was not dead (as had been reported) but only sleeping in the literal sense of the word? The crowd took him to mean that, but it was perfectly evident to them that she was dead: 'they laughed at him', say all three evangelists; 'knowing that she was dead', Luke adds (and the fact that he says 'knowing' rather than 'supposing' suggests that he believed that she had died). Or did Jesus mean that her state of death, though real, was not to be permanent – that it would prove to be nothing more than a temporary sleep? Did he, in other words, use the word 'sleep' figuratively, as he did when he reported the death of Lazarus to his disciples by saying, 'Our friend Lazarus has fallen asleep, but I go to awake him out of sleep' (John 11:11)? It is beside the point to say that two different Greek words for 'sleep' are used – one in the story of Jairus's daughter and the other in the Lazarus narrative. Both of them can be used figuratively for death in appropriate contexts.

Which way, then, should our Lord's words be taken? We cannot be sure, in the absence of the confirmation which a medical certificate would supply. To the modern reader his words are ambiguous. To the child he used the kind of language which might be used by anyone waking a child up from sleep: *Talitha cumi* is the Aramaic for 'Little girl, get up!' But the mere waking of a child from sleep is not the kind of action which would call for special commemoration: the fact that the evangelists record the incident, coupled with the way in which they record it, implies their belief that she was really (if only temporarily) dead.

6.

SALTLESS SALT

'Salt is good; but if the salt has lost its saltness, how will you season it?' (Mark 9:50)

One can use salt to season meat or bread, but if the salt that one might use for this purpose loses its saltness, what can be used to season *it*?

But how can salt lose its saltness? If it is truly salt, of course, it must remain salt and retain its saltness. But probably in the ordinary experience of Galilean life, salt was rarely found in a pure state; in practice it was mixed with other substances, various forms of earth. So long as the proportion of salt in the mixture was sufficiently high, the mixture would serve the purpose of true salt. But if, through exposure to damp or some other reason, all the salt in the mixture was leached out, what was left was good for nothing. As Luke, in his amplified version of the saying, puts it, 'it is fit neither for the land nor for the dunghill' (Luke 14:35). It might have been thought that the dunghill was all that it was fit for, but Jesus may have used a word that meant 'manure': 'it is no good for the land, not even as manure'. Matthew says, 'It is no longer good for anything except to be thrown out and trodden under foot by men' (Matt. 5:13); that is to say, people throw the useless stuff out into the street.

The figure of insipid salt appears in the words of the rabbis, with reference (it seems) to Israel's role as the salt or purifying agency among the nations of mankind. Matthew's version of Jesus's saying begins with the words: 'You are the salt of the earth' (Matt. 5:13) addressed to his disciples. This implies that the disciples have a particular function to perform on earth, and that, if they fail to perform it, they might as well not exist, for all the good they will do. In what respect they are said to be salt is not specified, so the nature of their function has to be inferred from the context and from what is known of the effect of salt. They may be intended to have a preserving and purifying effect on their fellows, or to add zest to the life of the community, or to be a force for peace. The idea of an insipid Christian ought to be a contradiction in terms. One way in which the quality of saltness can be manifested is in one's language. 'Let your speech be always gracious, seasoned with salt', Paul writes to the Colossians (Col. 4:6), where the 'salt' seems to be that ready Christian wit or wisdom (specially apt in the answering of questions about the faith) which is far removed from the slanderous and unsavoury talk deprecated earlier in the same letter (3:7).

Since the disciples are spoken of as the salt of the earth in the same context of the Sermon on the Mount in which they are also spoken of as the light of the world and a city set on a hill (Matt. 5:14), it is evidently their public life that is in view. They must be seen by others as living examples of the power and grace of God, examples which others are encouraged to follow.

Mark adds some other sayings in which salt figures. These 'salt' sayings follow the warning that it is better to enter into life maimed than to be consigned with all one's limbs to the 'Gehenna of fire' (Mark 9:43–48). A transition between that warning and the 'salt' sayings is provided by the sentence: 'For every one shall be salted with fire' (Mark 9:49). The fires which burned continuously in the Gehenna or municipal refuse-tip south of Jerusalem (see p. 51) reduced the risk of disease which might have arisen from the decomposing organic matter; fire had a purifying effect, as salt also had. The point of Jesus's words in this 'transitional' sentence may be that the fire of persecution will have a purifying or refining effect in the disciples' lives (cf. 1 Pet. 1:6–7). Some texts of Mark append here a quotation from Leviticus 2:13 (where the reference is more particularly to the cereal offering): 'and every sacrifice will be salted with salt'. This clause is probably not original in this context, but those who were responsible for inserting it (being moved to do so probably by the common theme of salt) may have intended it to mean: 'Every Christian, by enduring persecution, will be cleansed thereby and so become a more acceptable offering to God.'

Then, after the saying about the salt that has lost its saltness, Mark concludes this series of sayings with 'Have salt in yourselves, and be at peace with one another.' Again, we should understand this injunction better if we knew the situation in which it was originally spoken. 'Have salt in yourselves' might mean 'Have salt among yourselves' and might refer to the eating of salt together which was an expression of fellowship at table and therefore of peaceful relations. If this is so, then 'be at peace with one another' is a non-figurative explanation of 'have salt among yourselves'. But we cannot be sure.

7.

THE OLD IS BETTER

'And no one after drinking old wine desires new; for he says, "The old is good"' (Luke 5:39)

The ancient authorities for the text read variously 'The old is good' and 'The old is better', but even if we accept the authority of those which read 'The old is good', it makes no material difference: anyone who said, with reference to wine, 'The old is good' meant that it was better than the new wine.

This is not so much a hard saying as a misunderstood saying. It is often treated as though it carried Jesus's authority and could be applied to a wide variety of situations in which the old is threatened by the new – an old version of the Bible, an old form of worship, an old method of evangelism, and in short everything that is popularly summed up in the traditional term 'the old-time religion'. But Jesus quotes the saying; he does not necessarily endorse it. The saying is preserved by Luke, who appends it to his version of Jesus's words about new wine and old wineskins. In those words, taken over from Mark 2:22, Jesus compares his message of the kingdom of God to new wine, which cannot be contained in old wineskins that have lost their elasticity. The old wineskins were the rules and forms of traditional religion, which were menaced, as many religious people thought, by Jesus's revolutionary teaching. If, in the saying appended by Luke, the new wine has the same meaning – Jesus's message of the kingdom – then the people who say 'The old is good' or 'The old is better' are expressing their preference for the old, established, familiar ways. New teaching is disturbing; it forces people to think, to revise their ideas and attitudes. Religious people tend to be conservative, to suspect innovations. Job's friends were like this: the wisdom to which they appealed had the sanction of antiquity, and Job's arguments tended to upset it. 'What do you know that we do not know?' asked Eliphaz the Temanite. 'What do you understand that is not clear to us? Both the gray-haired and the aged are among us, older than your father' (Job 15:9–10).

Jesus found that much resistance to accepting his message, on the part not of hostile but of well-intentioned and pious people, arose simply from this attachment to old ways and old ideas. They had stood the test of time; why should they be changed? This was a perfectly natural response, and one which was not totally regrettable: it could be a safeguard against the tendency to fall for anything new just because it was new – to embrace novelty for novelty's sake. But when God does a new thing or imparts a new revelation, as he did in the ministry of Jesus, then this instinctive preference for the old could be an obstacle to the progress of his cause. Ultimately, the question to ask about any teaching is not 'Is it old?' or 'Is it new?' but 'Is it true?' Old wine has a goodness of its own and new wine has a goodness of its own. Personal preference there may be, but there is no room for the dogmatism which says, 'No wine is fit to drink till it is old.'

'The old is good' or 'The old is better', then, far from expressing the mind of Jesus, could well express an attitude which he deplores because it hinders the advance of the kingdom of God.

8.

ONE JOT OR ONE TITTLE SHALL IN NO WISE PASS

'Think not that I have come to abolish the law and the prophets; I have come not to abolish them but to fulfil them. For truly, I say to you, till heaven and earth pass away, not an iota, not a dot, will pass from the law until all is accomplished. Whoever then relaxes one of the least of these commandments, and teaches men so, shall be called least in the kingdom of heaven; but he who does them and teaches them shall be called great in the kingdom of heaven. For I tell you, unless your righteousness exceeds that of the scribes and Pharisees, you will never enter the kingdom of heaven' (Matt. 5:17–20)

Here is surely an uncompromising affirmation of the eternal validity of the law of Moses. Not the smallest part of it is to be abrogated. The 'jot' (AV) is the smallest letter of the Hebrew alphabet; the 'iota' (RSV) is the smallest letter of the Greek alphabet. The 'tittle' (AV) or 'dot' (RSV) was a very small mark attached to a letter, perhaps to distinguish it from another which resembled it, as in our alphabet 'G' is distinguished from 'C', or 'Q' from 'O'.

What is hard about this uncompromising affirmation? For some readers the hardness lies in the difficulty of recognising in this speaker the Christ who, according to Paul, 'is the end of the law, that every one who has faith may be justified' (Rom. 10:4).

Others find no difficulty in supposing that Paul's conception of Jesus differed radically from the presentation of his character and teaching in the Gospels. The view has indeed been expressed (not so frequently nowadays as at an earlier time) that Paul is pointed to as the man who 'relaxes one of the least of these commandments and teaches men so'. This implies that the saying does not come from Jesus, but from a group in the early Church which did not like Paul. Even where the reference to Paul would not be entertained, it is held by many that these words come from a group in the early Church which wished to maintain the full authority of the law for Christians. The saying, according to Rudolf Bultmann, 'records the attitude of the conservative Palestinian community in contrast to that of the Hellenists'.[1]

There were probably several selections of sayings of Jesus in circulation before the Gospels proper began to be produced, and one of these, which was preferred by stricter Jewish Christians, seems to have been used, along with others, by Matthew. Such a selection of sayings could be drawn up in accordance with the outlook of those who compiled it; sayings which in themselves appeared to support that outlook would be included, while others which appeared to go contrary to it would be omitted. The teaching of Jesus was much more diversified than any partisan selection of his sayings would indicate. By not confining himself to any one selection Matthew gives an all-round picture of the teaching. A saying such as has just been quoted had three successive life-settings: its life-setting in the historical ministry of Jesus, its setting in a restricted selection of Jesus's sayings, and its setting in the Gospel of Matthew. It is only its setting in the Gospel of Matthew that is immediately accessible to us. (In addition to these three settings, of course, it may have acquired subsequent life-settings in the history of the Church and in the course of interpretation. The statement 'I have come not to abolish them but to fulfil them' has been used, for example, to present the gospel as the crown of fulfilment of Hinduism,[2] but such a use of it is irrelevant to the intention of Jesus or of the evangelist.)

To the remark that it is only in its setting in the Gospel of

Matthew that the saying is immediately accessible to us there is a partial exception. Part of it occurs in a different context in the Gospel of Luke. In Luke 16:16-17 (between the parable of the unjust steward and the story of the rich man and Lazarus; see p. 116). Jesus says, 'The law and the prophets were until John; since then the good news of the kingdom of God is preached, and every one enters it violently. But it is easier for heaven and earth to pass away, than for one dot of the law to become void.' The second of these two sentences is parallel to (but not identical with) Matthew 5:18, the saying about the jot and tittle (or the iota and dot).

The selection of sayings which is supposed to have been drawn up in a more legally minded Christian circle, and which Matthew is widely considered to have used as one of his sources, is often labelled M (because it is represented in Matthew's Gospel only). Another, more comprehensive, selection on which both Matthew and Luke are widely considered to have drawn is commonly labelled Q. It may be, then, that the form of the 'jot and tittle' saying found in Matthew 5:18 is the M form, while that found in Luke 16:17 is the Q form. T. W. Manson was one scholar who believed that this was so, and he invited his readers to bear two possibilities in mind. The first possibility was that Luke's form of the saying is closer to the original wording and that the form in Matthew 'is a revision of it to bring it explicitly into line with Rabbinical doctrine'. The other possibility, which follows on from this one, was 'that the saying in its original form asserts not the perpetuity of the Law but the unbending conservatism of the scribes', that it is not intended to be 'sound Rabbinical dogma but bitter irony'. Jesus, that is to say, addresses the scribes and says, 'The world will come to an end before you give up the tiniest part of your traditional interpretation of the law.'[3]

It is plain that Jesus did not accept the rabbinical interpretation of the law. Indeed, he charged the scribes, the acknowledged students and teachers of the law, with 'transgressing the commandment of God for the sake of their tradition' (so the wording runs in Matthew 15:3, in a passage

based on Mark 7:9). He said that by their application of the law
'they bind heavy burdens, hard to bear, and lay them on men's
shoulders' (Matt. 23:4); by contrast, he issued the invitation:
'Take my yoke upon you, and learn from me; for . . . my yoke is
easy, and my burden is light' (Matt. 11:29-30).

But he did not relax the requirements of God's law as such,
nor did he recommend a lower standard of righteousness than
the 'scribes and Pharisees' required. On the contrary: he
insisted that admittance to the kingdom of heaven called for
righteousness exceeding that of the scribes and Pharisees. This
last statement, found in Matthew 5:20, serves as an
introduction to the paragraphs which follow, in which Jesus's
account of what obedience to the law involves is given in a
succession of hard sayings, at which we shall look one by one.
But at the moment we may mention two principles by which he
interpreted and applied the law.

First, he maintained that the proper way to keep any
commandment was to fulfil the purpose for which it was given.
He did this with regard to the law of marriage (see p. 58); he
did it also with regard to the sabbath law. On the sabbath day,
said the fourth commandment, 'you shall not do any work'. In
the eyes of some custodians of the law, this called for a careful
definition of what constituted 'work', so that people might
know precisely what might or might not be done on that day.
Circumstances could alter cases: an act of healing, for example,
was permissible if it was a matter of life and death, but if the
treatment could be put off to the following day without any
danger or detriment to the patient, that would be better. It was
precisely on this issue that Jesus collided repeatedly with the
scribes and their associates. His criterion for the keeping of this
law was to inquire for what purpose the sabbath was instituted.
It was instituted, he held, to provide rest and relief for human
beings: they were not made for the sake of the sabbath, but the
sabbath was given for their sake (see p. 33). Therefore, any
action which promoted their rest, relief and general well-being
was permissible on the sabbath. It was not merely permissible
on the sabbath: the sabbath was the most appropriate day for

its performance, because its performance so signally promoted God's purpose in instituting the sabbath. Jesus appears to have cured people by preference on the sabbath day, because such an action honoured the day.

He did not abrogate the fourth commandment: he interpreted it in a different way from the current interpretation. Did his principle of interpretation 'exceed the righteousness of the scribes and Pharisees?' Perhaps it did. There are some people who find it easier to have a set of rules: when a practical problem arises, they can consult the rules and know what to do. But if they have to decide which action best fulfils the purpose of the law, that involves thought, and thought of this kind, with the personal responsibility that accompanies it, is a difficult exercise for them.

Secondly, Jesus maintained that obedience or disobedience to the law began inwardly, in the human heart. It was not sufficient to conform one's outward actions and words to what the law required; the thought-life must be conformed to it first of all. One of the Old Testament psalmists voiced his feelings thus: 'I delight to do thy will, O my God; thy law is within my heart' (Ps. 40:8). This psalm is not quoted by Jesus in the Gospels, but in another place in the New Testament its language is applied to him (Heb. 10:7, 9). It does indeed express very well the attitude of Jesus himself and the attitude which he recommended to his hearers. Where the mind and will are set to do the will of God, the speaking and acting will not deviate from it.

Besides, where this is so, there will be an emphasis on the inward and spiritual aspects of ethics and religion, rather than on the outward and material aspects. The idea that a religious obligation could be given precedence over one's duty to one's parents was one with which Jesus had no sympathy (cf. Mark 7:10–13). This idea was approved by some exponents of the law in his day, but in general Jewish teaching has agreed with him here. Again, Jesus set very little store by details of ritual purification or food regulations, because these had no ethical content. Mark goes so far as to say that by his pronouncements on these last matters 'he declared all foods clean' (Mark 7:19). If Matthew does not reproduce these words of Mark, he does reproduce the pronouncements of Jesus which Mark so interprets (Matt. 15:17–20).

But did the ritual washings and food restrictions not belong to the jots and tittles of the law? Should they not be reckoned, at the lowest estimate, among 'the least of these commandments'? Perhaps so, but in Jesus's eyes 'justice, mercy and faith' were of much greater importance (Matt. 23:23). And what about the sacrificial ceremonies? They were included in the law, to be sure, but Jesus's attitude to such things is summed up in his quotation from a great Old Testament prophet: 'I desire mercy, and not sacrifice' (Hos. 6:6). It is Matthew, and Matthew alone among the evangelists, who records Jesus as quoting these words, and he records him as using them twice (Matt. 9:13; 12:7). The law is fulfilled ethically rather than ceremonially. Jesus confirmed the insistence of the great prophets that punctiliousness in ceremonial observances is worse than useless where people neglect 'to do justice, and to love kindness, and to walk humbly with ... God' (Mic. 6:8). It is human beings, and not inanimate things, that matter.

The law for Jesus was the expression of God's will. The will of God is eternal and unchangeable. Jesus did not come to modify the will of God; he fulfilled it. The standard of obedience to that will which he set, by his example and his teaching alike, is more exacting than the standard set by the written law. He insisted that the will of God should be done from the heart. But, in so insisting, he provided the means by which the doing of God's will from the heart should not be an unattainable ideal. If Paul may be brought in to interpret the teaching of Jesus here, the apostle who maintained that men and women are justified before God through faith in Jesus and not through keeping the law also maintained that those who have faith in Jesus receive his Spirit so that 'the just requirement of the law might be fulfilled in us, who walk not according to the flesh but according to the Spirit' (Rom. 8:4). The gospel demands more than the law, but supplies the power to do it. Someone has put it in doggerel but telling lines:

> To run and work the law commands,
> Yet gives me neither feet nor hands;
> But better news the gospel brings:
> It bids me fly, and gives me wings.

9.

'YOU FOOL!' MERITS HELL FIRE

'Every one who is angry with his brother shall be liable to judgment; whoever insults his brother shall be liable to the council, and whoever says, "You fool!" shall be liable to the hell of fire' (Matt. 5:22)

This is the first of a series of statements in which Jesus makes the requirements of the law more radical than the strict letter might indicate. Quoting the sixth commandment, Jesus says, 'You have heard that it was said to the men of old, "You shall not kill; and whoever kills shall be liable to judgment"'. 'But *I* say to you,' he continues, and then comes the passage above, ending in the hard saying about the penalty incurred by one who says to another, 'You fool!'

Murder was a capital offence under Israelite law; the death penalty could not be commuted to a monetary fine, such as was payable for the killing of someone's domestic animal. Where it could be proved that the killing was accidental – as when a man's axe-head flew off the handle and struck his fellow-workman on the head – it did not count as murder, but even so the owner of the axe-head had to take prudential measures to escape the vengeance of the dead man's next of kin. Otherwise, the killer was brought before the village elders and on the testimony of two or three witnesses was sentenced to death. The death penalty was carried out by stoning: the witnesses threw the first stones, and then the community joined in, thus dissociating themselves from blood-guiltiness and expiating the pollution which it brought on the place.

Jesus points out that the murderous act springs from the angry thought. It is in the mind that the crime is first committed and judgment is incurred. The earthly court cannot take action against the angry thought, but the heavenly court can – and does. This in itself is a hard saying. According to the AV, 'whosoever is angry with his brother without a cause shall be in danger of the judgment', but the phrase 'without a cause' is a later addition to the Greek text, designed to make Jesus's words more tolerable. The other man's anger may be sheer bad temper, but mine is righteous indignation – anger with a cause. Like the prophet Jonah, 'I do well to be angry' (Jonah 4:9). But Jesus's words, in the original form of the text, make no distinction between righteous and unrighteous anger: anyone who is angry with his brother exposes himself to judgment. There is no saying where unchecked anger may end. 'Be angry but do not sin', we are told in Ephesians 4:26; that is, 'If you are angry, do not let your anger lead you into sin; let sunset put an end to your anger, for otherwise it will provide the devil with an opportunity which he will not be slow to seize.'

There seems to be an ascending scale of seriousness as Jesus goes on: 'liable to judgment . . . liable to the council . . . liable to the hell of fire'. The council in question is the Sanhedrin, apparently the supreme court of the nation in contrast to a local court. Evidently, then, to insult one's brother is more serious than to be angry with him. This is clearly so: the angry thought can be checked, but the insult once spoken cannot be recalled and may cause violent resentment. The person insulted may retaliate with a fatal blow, for which in fact if not in law the victim of the blow may be as much to blame as the one who strikes it. The actual insult mentioned by Jesus is the word 'Raca', as it stands in the AV. The precise meaning of 'Raca' is disputed; it is probably an Aramaic word meaning something like 'imbecile' but was plainly regarded as a deadly insult. (Words of abuse are above all others to be avoided by speakers of a foreign language; they can have an unimagined effect on a native speaker of the language.)

But 'whoever says, "You fool!" shall be liable to the hell of fire'. From this we might gather that 'you fool!' is a deadlier insult than 'Raca', whatever 'Raca' may mean. For 'the hell of fire' (RSV) or 'hell fire' (AV) is the most severe penalty of all. The 'hell of fire' is the fiery Gehenna. Gehenna is the valley on the south side of Jerusalem which, after the return from the Babylonian exile, served as the city's rubbish dump and public incinerator. In earlier days it had been the site of the worship of Molech, and so it was thought fit that it should be degraded in this way. In due course it came to be used as a symbol of the destruction of the wicked after death, just as the garden of Eden became a symbol of the blissful paradise to be enjoyed by the righteous.

But was 'You fool!' actually regarded as being such a deadly insult? In this same Gospel of Matthew the cognate adjective is used of the man who built his house on the sand (7:26) and of the five girls who forget to take a supply of oil to keep their torches alight (25:2–3), and Jesus himself is reported as calling certain religious teachers 'blind fools' (23:17). It is more probable that, just as 'Raca' is a non-Greek word, so is the word *mōre* that Jesus used here. If so, then it is a word which to a Jewish ear meant 'rebel (against God)' or 'apostate'; it was the word which Moses in exasperation used to the disaffected Israelites in the wilderness of Zin: 'Hear now, you rebels; shall we bring forth water for you out of this rock?' (Num. 20:10). For these rash words, uttered under intense provocation, Moses was excluded from the promised land.

Whether this was the word Jesus had in mind or not, he certainly had in mind the kind of language that is bound to produce a murderous quarrel: chief responsibility for the ensuing bloodshed, he insisted, lies with the person who spoke the offending word. But behind the offending word lies the hostile thought. It is there that the guilty process starts; and if the hostile thought is not killed off as soon as the thinker becomes aware of it, then, although no earthly court may be in a position to take cognisance of it, that is what will be the first count in the indictment before the judgment-bar of God.

10.

ADULTERY IN THE HEART

'Every one who looks at a woman lustfully has already committed adultery with her in his heart' (Matt. 5:28)

This is another instance of Jesus's making the law more stringent by carrying its application back from the outward act to the inward thought and desire. The seventh commandment says, 'You shall not commit adultery' (Exod. 20:14). In the cultural context of the original Decalogue, this commandment forbade a man to have sexual relations with someone else's wife. To infringe this commandment was a capital offence; the penalty was stoning to death (as it still is in some parts of the Near and Middle East). Another commandment seems to carry the prohibition back beyond the overt act: the second clause of the tenth commandment says, 'You shall not covet your neighbour's wife' (Exod. 20:17), where his wife is mentioned among several items of his property. In a property context one might 'covet' someone else's wife not by way of a sexual urge but because of the social or financial advantages of being linked with her family.

However that may be, Jesus traces the adulterous act back to the lustful glance and thought, and says that it is there that the rot starts: it is there, therefore, that the check must be immediately applied. Otherwise, if the thought is cherished, or fed by fantasy, the commandment has already been broken. There may be significance in the fact that Jesus does not speak of someone else's wife but of 'a woman' in general. Parallels to this saying can be found in rabbinical literature.

Pope John Paul II excited some comment in 1981 by saying that a man could commit adultery in this sense with his own wife. Emil Brunner, in fact, had said something to very much the same effect over forty years before.[1] But there is nothing outrageous about such a suggestion. To treat any woman as a sex object, and not as a person in her own right, is sinful; all the more so, when that woman is one's own wife.

11.

PLUCKING OUT THE RIGHT EYE

'If your right eye causes you to sin, pluck it out and throw it away; it is better that you lose one of your members than that your whole body be thrown into hell' (Matt. 5:29)

This saying is not so hard in the RSV form in which it has just been quoted as it is in some older versions. The AV says, 'If thy right eye offend thee . . .', which is generally meaningless to readers today; the verb 'offend' no longer means 'trip up' or anything like that, which in literary usage it still did in 1611. Less excusable is the RV rendering, 'If thy right eye causeth thee to stumble . . .', because this introduced an archaism which was long since obsolete in 1881.

The RSV rendering, however, is more intelligible. It means, in effect: 'Don't let your eye lead you into sin.' How could it do that? By resting too long on an object of temptation. Matthew places this saying immediately after Jesus's words about adultery in the heart, and that is probably the original context, for it provides a ready example of how a man's eye could lead him into sin. In the most notable case of adultery in the Old Testament – King David's adultery with the wife of Uriah the Hittite – the trouble began when, late one afternoon, David from his palace roof *saw* the lady bathing (2 Sam. 11:2). Jesus says, 'Better pluck out your eye – even your right eye (as being presumably the more precious of the two) – than allow it to lead you into sin; it is better to enter into eternal life with one eye than to be thrown into Gehenna (as a result of that sin) with two.'

Matthew follows up this saying about the right eye with a similar one about the right hand. This strong assertion seems to have stayed with the hearers; it is repeated in Matthew 18:8–9 (in dependence on Mark 9:43–48), where the foot is mentioned in addition to the eye and the hand.

Shortly after the publication of William Tyndale's English New Testament, the attempt to restrict its circulation was defended on the ground that the simple reader might mistakenly take such language literally and 'pluck out his eyes, and so the whole realm will be full of blind men, to the great decay of the nation and the manifest loss of the King's grace; and thus by reading of the Holy Scriptures will the whole realm come into confusion'. So a preaching friar is said to have declared in a Cambridge sermon; but he met his match in Hugh Latimer who, in a sermon preached the following Sunday, said that simple people were well able to distinguish between literal and figurative terms. 'For example,' Latimer went on, 'if we paint a fox preaching in a friar's hood, nobody imagines that a fox is meant, but that craft and hypocrisy are described, which so often are found disguised in that garb.'[1]

In fact, it is not recorded that anyone ever mutilated himself because of these words in the Gospels. There is indeed the case of Origen, but if the story is true that he made himself a eunuch 'for the kingdom of heaven's sake', that was in response to another saying, at which we shall look later (p. 63).

12.

DIVORCE AND REMARRIAGE

'Whoever divorces his wife and marries another, commits adultery against her; and if she divorces her husband and marries another, she commits adultery'
(Mark 10:11–12)

This was felt to be a hard saying by the disciples who first heard it; it is no less a hard saying for many of their present-day successors.

Jesus was asked to give a ruling on a point of law which was debated in the Jewish schools. In Deuteronomy 24:1–4 there is a law which says in effect, 'When a man divorces his wife because he has found "some indecency" in her, and she is then married to someone else who divorces her in his turn, her former husband may not take her back to be his wife again.' This law, forbidding a man who has divorced his wife to marry her again after she has lived with a second husband, does not lay down the procedure for divorce; it assumes this procedure as already in being. Nowhere in the Old Testament law is there an explicit command about the divorce procedure, but in this context it is implied that to divorce a woman a man had to make a written declaration that she was no longer his wife: 'he writes her a bill of divorce and puts it in her hand and sends her out of his house' (Deut. 24:1). Elsewhere in the Old Testament divorce is disparaged as something unworthy: 'I hate divorce, says the Lord the God of Israel', according to the prophet Malachi (2:16).

But in Deuteronomy 24 it is assumed that a man may divorce his wife, and that he may do so on account of 'some indecency' or 'something shameful' (NEB) that he has found in her. The interpreters of the law around the time of our Lord, who were concerned not only with deciding what it meant but with applying it to contemporary life, paid special attention to this phrase. What, they asked, might be indicated by this 'indecency' or unseemliness which justified a man in divorcing his wife?

There were two main schools of thought: one which interpreted it stringently, another which interpreted it more broadly. The former school, which followed the direction of Shammai, a leading rabbi who lived a generation or so before Jesus, said that a man was authorised to divorce his wife if he married her on the understanding that she was a virgin and then discovered that she was not. There was, in fact, an enactment covering this eventuality in the law of Deuteronomy (22:13–21), and the consequences could be very serious for the bride if the evidence was interpreted to mean that she had had illicit sexual relations before marriage. This, then, was one school's understanding of 'some indecency'.

The other school, following the lead of Shammai's contemporary Hillel, held that 'some indecency' might include more or less anything which her husband found offensive. She could cease to 'find favour in his eyes' for a variety of reasons – if she served up badly cooked food, for example, or even (one rabbi said) because he found her less beautiful than some other woman. It should be emphasised that the rabbis who gave these 'liberal' interpretations were not moved by a desire to make divorce easy: they were concerned to state what they believed to be the meaning of a particular scripture.

It was against this background that Jesus was invited to say what he thought. The Pharisees who put the question to him were themselves divided over the matter. In Matthew's account of the incident, they asked him, 'Is it lawful to divorce one's wife for any cause?' (19:3). If his answer was 'Yes', they would want to know for what cause or causes, in his judgment, divorce was permissible. He gave them his answer and then, in private, expanded it for the benefit of his disciples who had heard it.

As usual, he bypassed the traditional interpretation of the rabbinical schools and appealed to the scriptures. 'What did Moses command you?' he asked. 'Moses', they replied (referring to Deuteronomy 24:1–4), 'allowed a man to write a certificate of divorce, and to put her away.' They rightly said 'Moses allowed', not 'Moses commanded'; the enactment to which they referred, as we have seen, took for granted the existing divorce procedure, and wove it into a commandment relating to a further contingency. But Jesus told them that it was 'for your hardness of heart' that 'Moses wrote you this commandment'. Then, as with the sabbath law so with the marriage law, he went back to first principles. 'From the beginning of creation', he said, '"God made them male and female." "For this reason a man shall leave his father and mother and be joined to his wife, and the two shall become one." So they are no longer two but one. What therefore God has joined together, let not man put asunder' (Mark 10:2–9).

Jesus reminds them of the biblical account of the institution of marriage. The marriage law must conform with the purpose for which marriage was instituted by God. It was instituted to create a new unity of two persons, and no provision was made for the dissolving of that unity. Jesus does not idealise marriage. He does not say that every marriage is made in heaven; he says that marriage itself is made in heaven – that is, instituted by God. To the question, 'Is it lawful for a man to divorce his wife?' his answer, in effect, is 'No; not for any cause.'

There is a feature of Jesus's answer to the Pharisees which could easily be overlooked. The stringent interpretation of the school of Shammai and the 'liberal' interpretation of the school of Hillel were both given from the husband's point of view. In the stringent interpretation it was the bride's virginity that had to be above suspicion; the bridegroom's chastity before marriage did not enter into the picture. As for the 'liberal' interpretation, it was liberal in the husband's interest, in that it permitted him to divorce his wife for a variety of reasons; so far as the wife's interest was concerned, it was most illiberal, for she had little opportunity of redress if her husband decided to divorce her within the meaning of the law as 'liberally' interpreted. What was true of these interpretations was true of the original legislation which they undertook to expound: it was because of the hardness of *men's* hearts that divorce was conceded. The law was unequally balanced to the disadvantage of women, and Jesus's ruling, with its appeal to the Creator's intention, had the effect of redressing this unequal balance. It is not surprising that women regularly recognised in Jesus one who was their friend and champion.

We may observe in passing that, in referring to the creation ordinance, Jesus combined a text from the creation narrative of Genesis 1 with one from the narrative of Genesis 2. In Genesis 1:27, when 'God created man in his own image', the 'man' whom he so created was humanity, comprising both sexes: 'male and female he created them'. And in Genesis 2:24, after the story of the formation of Eve from Adam's side, the narrator adds: 'This is why a man leaves his father and his mother and cleaves to his wife, and they become one flesh.' That may be the narrator's comment on the story, but Jesus quotes it as the word of God. It is by God's ordinance that the two become one; men are given no authority to modify that ordinance.

When the disciples asked Jesus to clarify his ruling, he reworded it in the two statements quoted at the head of this section. The second of the two statements refers to a situation not contemplated in the Old Testament law, which made no provision for a wife to divorce her husband and marry another man. It has therefore been thought that this second statement is a corollary added to Jesus's original ruling when Christianity had made its way into the Gentile world. In a number of Gentile law-codes it was possible for a wife to initiate divorce proceedings, as it was not under Jewish law. But at the time when Jesus spoke there was a recent *cause célèbre* in his own country, to which he could well have referred.

Less than ten years before, Herodias, a granddaughter of Herod the Great, who had been married to her uncle Herod Philip and lived with him in Rome, fell in love with another uncle, Herod Antipas, tetrarch of Galilee and Perea, when he paid a visit to Rome. In order to marry Antipas (as Antipas also desired), she divorced her first husband. She did so under Roman law, since she was a Roman citizen (like all members of the Herod family). For a woman to marry her uncle was not a breach of Jewish law, as it was commonly interpreted at that time, but it was certainly a breach of Jewish law for her to marry her husband's brother. John the Baptist was imprisoned by Herod Antipas for insisting that it was unlawful for him to be married to his brother's wife. Jesus named no names, but any reference at that time, either in Galilee or in Perea, to a woman divorcing her husband and marrying someone else was bound to make hearers think of Herodias. If the suggestion that she was living in adultery came to her ears, Jesus would incur her mortal resentment as surely as John the Baptist had done.

But it was his words about divorce and remarriage on a man's part that his disciples found hard to take. Could a man not get rid of his wife for *any* cause? It seemed not, according to the plain understanding of what Jesus said. No wonder then that in the course of time the hardness of men's hearts modified his ruling, as earlier it had modified the Creator's original intention.

In Matthew's version of this interchange, Jesus's ruling is amplified by the addition of a few words: 'whoever divorces his wife, *except for unchastity*, and marries another, commits adultery' (Matt. 19:9). The same exception appears in another occurrence of his ruling in this Gospel, in the Sermon on the Mount: 'every one who divorces his wife, *except on the ground of unchastity*, makes her an adulteress; and whoever marries a divorced woman commits adultery' (Matt. 5:32). The ruling in this latter form appears also in Luke 16:18, but without the exceptive clause; the exceptive clause is found in Matthew's Gospel only, and found twice over.

What is to be made of the exceptive clause? Is it an addition reflecting the hardness of men's hearts? Or is it an expansion stating the obvious – that if something is done which by its very nature dissolves the marriage bond, then the bond is dissolved?

Is it an attempt to conform Jesus's ruling to Shammai's interpretation – that if the bride is found to have had an illicit sexual relation before her marriage, her husband is entitled to put her away? All these suggestions have been ventilated. Most probable is the view that the exceptive clause is designed to adapt the ruling to the circumstances of the Gentile mission. If this is so, the term 'unchastity' has a technical sense, referring to sexual unions which, while they might be sanctioned by use and wont in some parts of the Gentile world, were forbidden by the marriage law of Israel. It is a matter of history that the Church's traditional marriage law, with its list of relationships within which marriage might not take place, was based on that of Israel. What was to be done if two people, married within such forbidden degrees, were converted from paganism to Christianity? In this situation the marriage might be dissolved.

Certainly the Gentile mission introduced problems which were not present in the context of Jesus's ministry. One of these problems cropped up in Paul's mission-field, and Paul introduced his own 'exceptive clause' to take care of it, although in general he took over Jesus's prohibition of divorce among his followers. Some of Paul's converts put to him the case of a man or woman, converted from paganism to Christianity, whose wife or husband walked out because of the partner's conversion and refused to continue the marriage relationship. In such a situation, said Paul, let the non-Christian partner go; do not have recourse to law or any other means to compel him or her to return. The deserted spouse is no longer bound by the marriage tie which has been broken in this way (see p. 132). Otherwise, he said, 'to the married I give charge, not I but the Lord, that the wife should not separate from her husband (but if she does, let her remain single or else be reconciled to her husband) – and that the husband should not divorce his wife' (1 Cor. 7:10–16).

Plainly Paul, a considerable time before Mark's Gospel was written, knew what Jesus had laid down on the subject of marriage and divorce, and knew it in the same sense as Mark's account. Like his Master, Paul treated women as persons and not as part of their husbands' property. But the disciples who first heard Jesus's ruling on the subject found it revolutionary, and not altogether welcome; it took them some time to reconcile themselves to it.

Is it wise to take Jesus's rulings on this or other practical issues and give them legislative force? Perhaps not. The trouble is that, if they are given legislative force, exceptive clauses are bound to be added to cover special cases, and arguments will be prolonged about the various situations which are, or are not, included in the terms of those exceptive clauses. It is better, probably, to let his words stand in their uncompromising rigour as the ideal at which his followers ought to aim. Legislation has to make provision for the hardness of men's hearts, but Jesus showed a more excellent way than the way of legislation and supplies the power to change the human heart and make his ideal a practical possibility.

13.

EUNUCHS FOR THE KINGDOM OF HEAVEN'S SAKE

'For there are eunuchs who have been so from birth, and there are eunuchs who have been made eunuchs by men, and there are eunuchs who have made themselves eunuchs for the sake of the kingdom of heaven. He who is able to receive this, let him receive it' (Matt. 19:12)

This saying occurs in Matthew's Gospel only: it comes immediately after his version of the saying about marriage and divorce, which we have just considered. When their Master ruled out the possibility of their getting rid of their wives by divorce, the disciples suggested that, in that case, it was better not to marry. To this he replied, 'Not all men can receive this precept, but only those to whom it is given' (Matt. 19:11). This means that the only men who can successfully live a celibate life are those who have received the gift of celibacy. This context shows how the following reference to eunuchs is to be understood; it certainly shows how Matthew understood it.

The saying, as reproduced by Matthew, consists of three parts. The first two present no problem. Some men are born eunuchs, and as for being 'made eunuchs by men', that was no unfamiliar practice in the ancient Near East. The hard saying is the third part: what is meant by making oneself a eunuch 'for the sake of the kingdom of heaven'?

It is reported that one eminent scholar in the early Church, Origen of Alexandria (A.D. 185–254), took these words with

literal seriousness in the impetuousness of youth, and
performed the appropriate operation on himself.[1] In later life
he knew better: in his commentary on Matthew's Gospel he
rejects the literal interpretation of the words, while acknowledging that he once accepted it, and says that they should be
understood spiritually and not 'according to the flesh and the
letter'.

What then did Jesus mean? These words are no more to be
taken literally than his words about cutting off the hand or foot
or plucking out the eye that leads one into sin. In the Jewish
culture in which he lived and taught, marriage was the accepted
norm, and celibacy was not held in the high esteem which it
later came to enjoy in many parts of the Church. That men such
as John the Baptist and himself should deny themselves the
comforts of marriage and family life may well have aroused
comment, and here is his answer to unspoken questions. Some
men and women have abstained from marriage in order to
devote themselves more wholeheartedly to the cause of the
kingdom of heaven. The man who marries and brings up a
family incurs special responsibilities for his wife and children:
they have a major claim on his attention. Jesus indicated his
attitude towards the ties of the family into which he was born
when he said that anyone who did the will of God was his
brother, sister or mother (Mark 3:35). It was people like these –
those who had taken on themselves the yoke of the kingdom
which he proclaimed – who constituted his true family. To
incur the more restricted obligations which marriage and the
rearing of children involved would have limited his dedication
to the ministry to which he knew himself called.

At the same time, he made it plain that only a minority
among his followers could 'receive' this course: for most of
them marriage and family life should be the norm.

Twenty-five years later the same teaching was repeated in
different language by Paul. Paul himself found the celibate way
of life congenial, but knew that the consequences would be
disastrous if those who were not called to it tried to follow it.
Hence his advice for the majority of his converts was that 'each
man should have his own wife and each woman her own

husband' – for, as he went on to say, 'each has his own special gift from God, one of one kind and one of another' (1 Cor. 7:2, 7). Those whom God called to the celibate life would receive from him the 'gift' of celibacy – of making themselves 'eunuchs for the sake of the kingdom of heaven'.

14.

DO NOT SWEAR AT ALL

'But I say to you, "Do not swear at all"' (Matt. 5:34)

Perjury is a serious offence in any law-code. It was so in the law of Moses. Perjury is forbidden in the third commandment: 'You shall not take the name of the Lord your God in vain; for the Lord will not hold him guiltless who takes his name in vain' (Exod. 20:7). To swear an oath falsely in the name of God was a sin not only against the name but against the very person of God. Later the scope of the commandment was broadened to include any light or thoughtless use of the divine name, to the point where it was judged safest not to use it at all. That is why the name of the God of Israel, commonly spelt Yahweh, came to be called the ineffable name, because it was forbidden to pronounce it. The public reader in the synagogue, coming on this name in the scripture lesson, put some other form in its place, lest he should 'take the name of the Lord his God in vain' by saying 'Yahweh' aloud. But originally it was perjury that was in view in the commandment, and in other injunctions to the same effect from Exodus to Deuteronomy. Summing up the sense of those injunctions, Jesus said, 'You have heard that it was said to the men of old, "You shall not swear falsely, but shall perform to the Lord what you have sworn"' (Matt. 5:33).

Realising the seriousness of swearing by God if the truth of the statement was not absolutely sure, people tended to replace the name of God by something else – by heaven, for example – with the idea that a slight deviation from the truth would then be less unpardonable. From another passage in this Gospel

(Matt. 23:16–22) it may be gathered that there were some casuists who ruled that vows were more binding or less binding according to the precise wording of the oath by which they were sworn. This, of course, would be ethical trifling.

It was necessary that people should be forbidden to swear falsely, whether in the name of God or by any other form of words. 'Pay what you vow', says the Preacher whose practical maxims enrich the Old Testament Wisdom literature; 'it is better that you should not vow than that you should vow and not pay' (Eccles. 5:4–5). But Jesus recommends a higher standard to his disciples. 'Do not swear at all,' he says; 'let what you say be simply "Yes" or "No"; anything more than this comes from evil' (Matt. 5:37). An echo of these words is heard in a later book of the New Testament: 'But above all, my brethren, do not swear, either by heaven or by earth or with any other oath, but let your yes be yes and your no be no, that you may not fall under condemnation' (James 5:12).

The followers of Jesus should be known as men and women of their word. If they are known to have a scrupulous regard for truth, then what they say will be accepted without the support of any oath. This is not mere theory; it is well established in experience. One body of Jesus's followers, the Society of Friends, has persisted in applying these words of his literally. And such is their reputation for probity that most people would more readily trust the bare word of a Friend than the sworn oath of many another person. 'Anything more than this', said Jesus, 'comes of evil'; that is to say, the idea that a man or woman can be trusted to speak the truth only when under oath (if then) springs from dishonesty and suspicion, and tends to weaken mutual confidence in the exchanges of everyday life. No one demands an oath from those whose word is known to be their bond; even a solemn oath on the lips of others tends to be taken with a grain of salt.

15.

TURNING THE OTHER CHEEK

'If any one strikes you on the right cheek, turn to him the other also' (Matt. 5:39)

This is a hard saying in the sense that it prescribes a course of action which does not come naturally to us. Unprovoked assault prompts resentment and retaliation. If one wants to be painfully literal, the assault is particularly vicious, for if the striker is right-handed, it is with the back of his hand that he hits the other on the right cheek.

This is one of a number of examples by which Jesus shows that the life-style of the kingdom of God is more demanding than what the law of Moses laid down. 'You have heard that it was said, "An eye for an eye and a tooth for a tooth"' (Matt. 5:38). This was indeed laid down in Israel's earliest law-code (Exod. 21:24), and when it was first said it marked a great step forward, for it imposed a strict limitation on the taking of vengeance. It replaced an earlier system of justice according to which, if a member of tribe X injured a member of tribe Y, tribe Y was under an obligation to take vengeance on tribe X. This quickly led to a blood feud between the two tribes and resulted in suffering which far exceeded the original injury. But incorporated into Israel's law-code was the principle of exact retaliation: one eye, and no more, for an eye; one life, and no more, for a life. When wounded honour was satisfied with such precisely proportionate amends, life was much less fraught with hazards. The acceptance of this principle made it easier to regard monetary compensation as being, in many cases, a reasonable replacement for the infliction of an equal and opposite injury on the offending party.

But now Jesus takes a further step. 'Don't retaliate at all', he says to his disciples. 'Don't harbour a spirit of resentment; if someone does you an injury or puts you to inconvenience, show yourself master of the situation by doing something to his advantage. If he gets some pleasure out of hitting you, let him hit you again.' (It should not be necessary to say that this saying is no more to be pressed literally than the saying about plucking out one's right eye and throwing it away – see p. 54; it is not difficult to envisage the other cheek being turned in a very provocative manner.) If a soldier or other government official conscripts your services to carry a load for him so far, you are under compulsion; you are forced to do it. But, when you have reached the end of the stipulated distance, you are a free person again; then you can say to him, 'If you'd like it carried farther, I will gladly carry it for you.' The initiative has now become yours, and you can take it not by voicing a sense of grievance at having been put to such inconvenience but by performing an act of grace. This way of reacting to violence and compulsion is the way of Christ.

To have one's services conscripted to carry a soldier's pack for him is not an everyday experience in the Western world. How, in our situation, could this particular injunction of Jesus be applied? Perhaps when a citizen is directed by a policeman to assist him in the execution of his duty. But if (say) it is a matter of helping him to arrest a larger number of suspicious characters than he can cope with single-handed, would they not also come within the scope of duty to one's neighbour? This simply reminds us that Jesus's injunctions are not usually of the kind that can be carried out automatically; they often require careful thought. Whatever sacrifices he expects his followers to make, he does not ask them to sacrifice their minds. What they are urged to do is to have their minds conformed to his, and when careful thought is exercised in accordance with the mind of Christ, the resulting action will be in accordance with the way of Christ.

Another parallel might be the Christian's reaction to his

income tax demand. (Some followers of Christ have taken his teaching about property so seriously that they have no income on which tax can be paid – see p. 174.) The tax demanded must be paid; no choice can be exercised there. But suppose the Christian taxpayer, as an act of grace, pays double the amount demanded, or at least adds a substantial amount to it: what then? The computer would probably record it as tax overpaid, and the surplus would come back to him as a rebate. Perhaps it would be wisest if he were to send it direct to the Chancellor of the Exchequer, and send it anonymously – not only so as not to let his left hand know what his right hand was doing, but to forestall unworthy suspicions and enquiries. Once again, the carrying out of the simple injunctions of Jesus in a complex society like ours is not so easy. But where the spirit which he recommended is present, the performance should not go too far astray.

The admonition to turn the other cheek is given by Jesus to his disciples. It belongs to the sphere of personal behaviour. There are many Christians, however, who hold that this teaching should be put into practice by communities and nations as well as by individuals. Where Christian communities are concerned, we may well agree. The spectacle of the Church enlisting the aid of the 'secular arm' to promote its interests is rarely an edifying one. 'It belongs to the church of God', someone once said, 'to receive blows rather than to inflict them – but,' he added 'she is an anvil that has worn out many hammers.'[1] But what about a political community?

The situation did not arise in New Testament times. The first disciples of Jesus did not occupy positions of authority. Joseph of Arimathea might be an exception: he was a member of the Sanhedrin, the supreme court of the Jewish nation, and according to Luke (23:50–51), he did not go along with his colleagues' adverse verdict on Jesus. As the gospel spread into the Gentile world, some local churches included in their membership men who occupied positions of municipal responsibility, like Erastus, the city treasurer of Corinth (Rom. 16:23); but neither Paul nor any other New Testament writer finds it necessary to give special instructions to Christian rulers corresponding to those given to Christian subjects. But what was to happen when Christians became rulers, as in due course some did? Can the Christian magistrate practise non-retaliation towards the criminal who comes up before him for judgment? Could the Christian king practise non-retaliation towards a neighbouring king who declared war against him?

Paul, who repeats and underlines Jesus's teaching of non-retaliation, regards retaliation as part of the duty of the civil ruler. 'Would you have no fear of him who is in authority?' he asks. 'Then do what is good, and you will receive his approval, for he is God's servant for your good. But if you do wrong, be afraid, for he does not bear the sword in vain; he is the servant of God to execute his wrath on the wrongdoer' (Rom. 13:3-4). For Paul, the ruler in question was the Roman emperor or someone who held executive or judicial authority under him. But his words were relevant to their chronological setting. The time had not yet come (although it did come in less than ten years after those words were written) when the empire was openly hostile to the Church. Still less had the time come when the empire capitulated to the Church and emperors began to profess and call themselves Christians. When they inherited the 'sword' which their pagan predecessors had not borne 'in vain', how were they to use it? The answer to that question cannot be read easily off the pages of the New Testament. It is still being asked, and it is right that it should; but no single answer can claim to be the truly Christian one.

16.

LOVE YOUR ENEMIES

'But I say to you, "Love your enemies and pray for those who persecute you"' (Matt. 5:44)

Agreed, then: we should resist the impulse to pay someone who harms us back in his own coin, but does that involve *loving* him? Can we be expected to love to order?

Jesus's command to his disciples to love their enemies follows immediately on his words: 'You have heard that it was said, "You shall love your neighbour and hate your enemy"' (Matt. 5:43). 'You shall love your neighbour' is a quotation from the Old Testament law; it is part of what Jesus elsewhere referred to as the second of the two great commandments: 'You shall love your neighbour as yourself' (Lev. 19:18). On this commandment, with its companion 'You shall love the Lord your God ...' (Deut. 6:5), which he called 'the great and first commandment', Jesus said that all the law and the prophets depend (Matt. 22:36–40). But the commandment does not in fact go on to say 'You shall hate your enemy.' However, if it is only our neighbours that we are to love, and the word 'neighbours' be defined fairly narrowly, then it might be argued that we are free to hate those who are not our neighbours. But Jesus said, 'No; love your enemies as well as your neighbours.'

One difficulty lies in the sentimental associations that the word 'love' has for many of us. The love of which the law and the gospel alike speak is a very practical attitude: 'Let us not love in word or speech [only] but in deed and in truth' (1 John 3:18). Love to one's neighbour is expressed in lending him a helping hand when that is what he needs: 'Right,' says Jesus, 'lend your *enemy* a helping hand when that is what *he* needs. Your feelings towards him are not the important thing.'

But if we think we should develop more Christian feelings towards an enemy, Jesus points the way when he says 'Pray for those who persecute you' (or, as it is rendered in Luke 6:28, 'Pray for those who abuse you'). Those who have put this injunction into practice assure us that persistence in prayer for someone whom we don't like, however much it goes against the grain to begin with, brings about a remarkable change in attitude. Alexander Whyte quotes from an old diary the confessions of a man who had to share the same house and the same table with someone whom he found unendurable. He betook himself to prayer, until he was able to write, 'Next morning I found it easy to be civil and even benevolent to my neighbour. And I felt at the Lord's Table today as if I would yet live to love that man. I feel sure I will.'[1]

The best way to destroy an enemy is to turn him into a friend. Paul, who in this regard (as in so many others) reproduces the teaching of Jesus, sums it up by saying, 'Do not be overcome by evil, but overcome evil with good' (Rom. 12:21). He reinforces it by quoting from Prov. 25:21–22: 'If your enemy is hungry, feed him; if he is thirsty, give him drink; for by so doing you will heap burning coals upon his head'. Whatever that proverb originally meant, Paul adapts it to his purpose by omitting the self-regarding clause which follows those he quotes: 'and the Lord will reward you'. In this new context the 'burning coals' may mean the sense of shame which will be produced in the enemy, leading to a change of heart on his side too. But first do him a good turn; the feelings can be left to their own good time.

17.

YOU MUST BE PERFECT

'You, therefore, must be perfect, as your heavenly Father is perfect' (Matt. 5:48)

Some students of Christian ethics make a distinction between the general standards of Christian conduct and what are called 'counsels of perfection', as though the former were prescribed for the rank and file of Christians while the latter could be attained by real saints (see p. 174).

Such a distinction was not made by Jesus himself. He did make a distinction between the ordinary standards of morality observed in the world and the standard at which his disciples should aim; but the latter was something which should characterise all his disciples and not just a select few. For example, the principle that one good turn deserves another was observed by quite irreligious people and even by pagans. For anyone to repay a good turn with a bad one would be regarded as outrageous. But Jesus's followers were not to remain content with conventional standards of decent behaviour. According to conventional standards one good turn might deserve another, but according to the standards which he laid down for his disciples one bad turn deserves a good one – except that 'deserves' is not the right word. One bad turn may deserve a bad one in revenge, but one bad turn done to his disciples should be repaid by them with a good one. They must 'go the second mile'; they must do more than others do if they are to be known as followers of Jesus. If you confine your good deeds to your own kith and kin, he said to them, 'what more are

you doing than others? Do not even the Gentiles do the same?'
(Matt. 5:47). It is immediately after that that the words come:
'You, therefore, must be perfect, as your heavenly Father is
perfect.'

This indeed sounds like a 'counsel of perfection' in the most
literal sense. 'Be perfect like God.' Who can attain perfection
like his? Is it worthwhile even to begin to try? But the context
helps us to understand the force of these words. Why should
the disciples of Jesus, the heirs of the kingdom of God, repay
evil with good? The ancient law might say, 'You shall love your
neighbour as yourself' (Lev. 19:18), but the fulfilment of that
commandment depends on the answer given to the question,
'Who is my neighbour?' (Luke 10:29). When Jesus was asked
that question, he told the story of the good Samaritan to show
that my 'neighbour' in the sense intended by the commandment
is anyone who needs my help, anyone to whom I can render a
'neighbourly' service. But those Israelites to whom the
commandment was first given might not have thought of a
Canaanite as being a 'neighbour' within the meaning of the act,
and their descendants in New Testament times might not have
thought of a Roman in this way.

Most systems of ethics emphasise one's duty to one's
neighbour, but progress in ethics is marked by the broadening
scope indicated in the answer to the question 'Who is my
neighbour?' Why should I be neighbourly to someone who is
unneighbourly to me? If someone does me a bad turn, why
should I not pay him back in his own coin? Because, said Jesus,
God himself sets us an example in this regard. 'Your Father
who is in heaven ... makes his sun rise on the evil and on the
good, and sends rain on the just and on the unjust' (Matt. 5:45).
He bestows his blessings without discrimination. The followers
of Jesus are children of God, and they should manifest the
family likeness by doing good to all, even to those who deserve
the opposite. So, said Jesus, go the whole way in doing good,
just as God does.

The same injunction appears in a similar context, but in
slightly different words, in Luke 6:36, 'Be merciful, even as
your Father is merciful.' When we find one and the same saying

preserved in different forms by two evangelists, as we do here, the reason often is that Jesus's Aramaic words have been translated into Greek in two different ways. We do not know the precise Aramaic words that Jesus used on this occasion, but they probably meant, 'You must be perfect (that is, all-embracing, without any restriction) in your acts of mercy or kindness, for that is what God is like.'

When the books of the law were read in synagogue from the original Hebrew, the reading was accompanied by an oral paraphrase (called a *targum*) in Aramaic, the popular vernacular. There is a passage in the law (Lev. 22:26-28) which prescribes kindness to animals. In one of the Aramaic paraphrases, this passage ended with the words: 'As our Father is merciful in heaven, so you must be merciful on earth.' Perhaps, then, some of Jesus's hearers recognised a familiar turn of phrase when this 'hard saying' fell from his lips. It is not, after all, hard to understand; it is sometimes hard to practise it.

18.

IF YOU DO NOT FORGIVE YOUR BROTHER

'So also my heavenly Father will do to every one of you, if you do not forgive your brother from your heart' (Matt. 18:35)

This is a very hard saying. The 'so' which introduces it refers to the severe punishment which the king in a parable inflicted on an unforgiving servant of his. The parable arises out of a conversation between Jesus and Peter. Jesus repeatedly impressed on his disciples the necessity of forgiveness: they were not to harbour resentment, but freely forgive those who injured them. 'Yes, but how often?' Peter asked. 'Seven times?' – and probably he thought that that was about the limit of reasonable forbearance. 'Not seven times,' said Jesus, 'but seventy times seven' (Matt. 18:21–22). Perhaps by the time one had forgiven for the seventy-times-seventh time, forgiveness would have become second nature to one.

Some commentators have seen an allusion here to the war-song of Lamech in Genesis 4:24. Lamech was a descendant of Cain, who (surprisingly, it may be thought) was taken under God's protection. 'If any one slays Cain,' said God, 'vengeance shall be taken on him sevenfold.' Lamech boasted in his war-song that no one would injure him and get away with it: 'If Cain is avenged sevenfold, truly Lamech seventy-sevenfold' (or perhaps 'seventy times sevenfold'). Over against seventy-times-sevenfold vengeance Jesus sets, as the target for his followers, seventy-times-sevenfold forgiveness.

The gospel is a message of forgiveness: it could not be otherwise, because it is the gospel of God, and God is a forgiving God. 'Who is a God like thee, pardoning iniquity?' said one Hebrew prophet (Mic. 7:18). 'I knew', said another (protesting against God's proneness to forgive those who, he thought, did not deserve forgiveness), 'that thou art a gracious God and merciful, slow to anger, and abounding in steadfast love' (Jonah 4:2). It is to be expected, then, that those who receive the forgiveness which God holds out in the gospel, those who call him their Father, will display something of his character and show a forgiving attitude to others. If they do not, what then?

What then? Jesus answers this question in the parable of the unforgiving servant, which he told to confirm his words to Peter about repeated forgiveness 'until seventy times seven'. A king, said Jesus, decided to settle accounts with his servants, and found that one of them (who must have been a very high officer of state) had incurred debts to the royal exchequer which ran into millons. The king was about to deal with him as an oriental potentate might be expected to do, when the man fell at his feet, begged for mercy, and promised that, if the king would be patient with him, he would make full repayment. The king knew perfectly well that he could never repay such a debt, but he felt sorry for him and remitted the debt. Then the man found someone else in the royal service who was in debt to him personally (not to the king): his debt amounted to a few pounds. He demanded prompt repayment, and when this debtor asked for time to pay he refused and had him consigned to the debtors' prison. The king got to hear of it, and summoned the man whom he had pardoned back into his presence, revoked the pardon, and treated him as he had treated the other: 'In anger his lord delivered him to the jailers, till he should pay all his debt'. 'So,' said Jesus, 'in this way my heavenly Father will deal with any one of you if you do not forgive your brother (or sister) from your heart.' Revoke a pardon once granted? God would not do a thing like that, surely? Jesus said he would. A hard saying indeed!

That this emphasis on the necessity of having a forgiving

spirit had a central place in the teaching of Jesus is evident from the fact that it is enshrined in both versions of the Lord's Prayer. In Luke 11:4 the disciples are told to pray, 'Forgive us our sins, for we ourselves forgive every one who is indebted to us.' It is difficult to believe that anyone could utter this prayer deliberately, knowing at the same time that he or she cherished an unforgiving spirit towards someone else. In the Aramaic language which Jesus spoke the word for 'sin' is the same as the word for 'debt'; hence 'every one who is indebted to us' means 'everyone who has sinned against us'. In the parallel petition of Matthew 6:12 this use of 'debt' in the sense of 'sin' occurs twice: 'Forgive us our debts, as we also have forgiven our debtors' means 'Forgive us our sins, as we for our part have forgiven those who have sinned against us.' This wording implies that the person praying has already forgiven any injury received; otherwise it would be impossible honestly to ask God's forgiveness for one's own sins. Immediately after Matthew's version of the prayer this is emphasised again: 'For if you forgive men their trespasses, your heavenly Father also will forgive you; but if you do not forgive men their trespasses, neither will your Father forgive your trespasses' (Matt. 6:14–15).

The meaning is unambiguous, and it is unwise to try to avoid its uncomfortable challenge. One well-known annotated edition of the Bible had a comment on the clause 'as we forgive our debtors' which ran as follows: 'This is legal ground. Cf. Eph. 4.32, which is grace. Under law forgiveness is conditioned upon a like spirit in us; under grace we are forgiven for Christ's sake, and exhorted to forgive because we have been forgiven.'[1] But forgiveness is neither given nor received on 'legal ground'; it is always a matter of grace. What Paul says in Ephesians 4:32 is this: 'Be kind to one another, tenderhearted, forgiving one another, as God in Christ forgave you.' But if some of those to whom this admonition was addressed (and it is addressed to all Christians at all times) should persist in an unforgiving attitude towards others, could they even so enjoy the assurance of God's forgiveness? If Jesus's teaching means what it says, they could not.

Jesus told another parable about two debtors to illustrate another aspect of forgiveness. This was in the house of Simon the Pharisee, who neglected to pay him the courtesies normally shown to a guest, whereas the woman who ventured in from the street lavished her grateful affection on him by wetting his feet with her tears (Luke 7:36–50; see p. 29). The point of the parable was that one who has been forgiven a great debt will respond with great love, whereas no great response will be made by one whose sense of having been forgiven is minimal. (It might be objected that the man who had been forgiven a colossal debt in the parable in Matthew 18:23–35 showed little love in return, but the two parables are addressed to two different situations, and forgiveness and love are not subject to cast-iron rules of inevitable necessity.) Where there is a genuine response of love, there will be a forgiving spirit, and where there is a forgiving spirit, there will be a still greater appreciation of God's forgiving mercy, and still greater love in consequence. Some commentators find difficulty with Jesus's words about the woman, 'Her sins, which are many, are forgiven; for she loved much': the logic of the parable would suggest 'She loves much, for her sins have been forgiven'. But if that had been the meaning, that is what would have been said. Love and forgiveness set up a chain reaction: the more forgiveness, the more love; the more love, the more forgiveness.

19.

LEAD US NOT INTO TEMPTATION

'And lead us not into temptation' (Matt. 6:13; Luke 11:4)

The traditional rendering of the Lord's Prayer in English contains as its second-last petition, 'And lead us not into temptation'. It is a petition which has puzzled successive generations of Christians, for whom the word 'temptation' ordinarily means temptation to sin. Why should we ask God not to lead us into this? As if God would do any such thing! 'God cannot be tempted with evil and he himself tempts no one' (James 1:13).

Perhaps this was absolutely the last petition in the original form of the Lord's Prayer, as it is to this day in the authentic text of Luke's version. The petition which follows it in the traditional rendering, 'but deliver us from evil', found in Matthew's version, was perhaps added to help to explain the preceding one – whether the added petition means 'Deliver us from what is evil' or 'Deliver us from the evil one'. Is God asked to deliver his children from evil by preserving them *from* temptation or by preserving them *in* temptation? By preserving them *in* temptation, probably. It is appropriate to be reminded of a very similar petition which occurs in the Jewish service of morning and evening prayer: 'Do not bring us into *the power of* temptation.' That seems to mean, 'When we find ourselves surrounded by temptation, may we not be overpowered by it.'

Temptation, when the word occurs in the older versions of the Bible, means more than temptation to sin: it has the wider

sense of testing. God 'tempts no one', according to James 1:13;
yet the same writer says, according to the AV, 'Count it all joy
when ye fall into divers temptations' and 'Blessed is the man
that endureth temptation' (James 1:2, 12). What he means is
simply brought out by the RSV: 'Count it all joy ... when you
meet various trials, for you know that the testing of your faith
produces steadfastness' and 'Blessed is the man who endures
trial, for when he has stood the test he will receive the crown of
life which God has promised to those who love him.' To the
same effect other Christians are assured in 1 Peter 1:6–7 that
the purpose of their being called to undergo various trials –
'manifold temptations' in the AV – is 'so that the genuineness of
your faith ... may redound to praise and glory and honour at
the revelation of Jesus Christ'. That is to say, when faith is
tested it is strengthened, and the outcome is reinforced stability
of character.

It was so in Old Testament times. When the AV of Genesis
22:1 says that 'God did tempt Abraham', the meaning is that he
tested him – tested his faith, that is to say. An untested faith is a
weak faith, compared with one that has passed through a
searching test and emerged victorious.

Jesus himself was led into 'temptation'. So Matthew implies
when he says (4:1) that 'Jesus was led up by the Spirit into the
wilderness to be tempted by the devil'. Mark (1:12) uses an even
stronger verb: after Jesus's baptism, he says, 'the Spirit
immediately drove him out into the wilderness'. What was the
nature of his 'temptation'? It was the testing of his faith in God,
the testing of his resolution to accept the path which he knew to
be his Father's will for him in preference to others which might
have seemed more immediately attractive. It was from that
testing that he returned – 'in the power of the Spirit', says Luke
(4:14) – to undertake his public ministry.

So, whatever is meant by the petition, 'Lead us not into
temptation', it is highly unlikely that it means 'Do not let our
faith be tested' or, as the NEB puts it, 'Do not bring us to the
test'. 'Do not bring us to the test' is at least as obscure as 'Lead
us not into temptation'. It invites the question: 'What test?'

Perhaps Paul had this petition in his mind when he says to

his friends in Corinth, 'No temptation has overtaken you that is not common to man. God is faithful, and he will not let you be tempted beyond your strength, but with the temptation will also provide the way of escape, that you may be able to endure it' (1 Cor. 10:13). This could well be regarded as an expansion of our problem petition, which unpacks its concentrated meaning. It was evidently so regarded by those whose thought lies behind the fifth-century Eastern *Liturgy of St. James*. In this liturgy the celebrant, after reciting the Lord's Prayer, goes on:

Yes, O Lord our God,
lead us not into temptation which we are not able to bear,
but with the temptation grant also the way out,
so that we may be able to remain steadfast;
and deliver us from evil.

This implies something like the following as the intention of our petition. We know that our faith needs to be tested if it is to grow strong; indeed, the conditions of life in this world make it inevitable that our faith must be tested. But some tests are so severe that our faith could not stand up to the strain; therefore we pray not to be brought into tests of such severity. If our faith gave way under the strain, that might involve us in moral disaster; it would also bring discredit on the name of the God whom we call our Father.

When we use the prayer, we may generalise this petition along these lines. But in the context of Jesus's ministry and his disciples' association with him, the petition may have had a more specific reference. What that reference was may be inferred from his admonition to some of his disciples in Gethsemane just before his arrest: 'Watch and pray that you may not enter into temptation' (Mark 14:38). When some regard is paid to the Aramaic wording which probably lies behind the evangelist's Greek rendering of the admonition, there is much to be said for the view of some scholars that it meant, 'Keep awake, and pray not to fail in the test!' The disciples had no idea how crucial was the test which was almost

upon them. It was the supreme test for him; what about them?
Would they, who had continued with their Master in his trials
thus far, stand by him in the imminent hour of ultimate trial, or
would they fail in the test? We know what happened: they
failed – temporarily, at least. Mercifully (for the world's
salvation was at stake), he did not fail. When the Shepherd was
struck down, the sheep were scattered. But he endured the
ordeal of suffering and death and, when he came back to life, he
gathered his scattered followers together again, giving them a
new start – and this time they did not fail in the test.

Our perspective on the events of Gethsemane and Calvary,
even when our lives are caught up into those events and
revolutionised by them, is necessarily different from theirs at
that time. Jesus was prepared for the winding up of the old age
and the breaking in of the new – the powerful coming of the
kingdom of God. The transition from the old to the new would
involve unprecedented tribulation, the birthpangs of the new
creation, which would be a test too severe even for the faith of
the elect, unless God intervened and cut it short. This
tribulation would fall pre-eminently on the Son of man, and on
his endurance of it the bringing in of the new age depended. He
was ready to absorb it in his own person, but would he find one
or two others willing to share it with him? James and John had
professed their ability to drink his cup and share his baptism,
but in the moment of crisis they, with their companions,
proved unequal to the challenge.

Going back, then, from our Lord's admonition in Gethsemane to the problem petition which we are considering, we
may conclude that in the context of Jesus's ministry its
meaning was, 'Grant that we may not fail in the test' – 'Grant
that the test may not prove too severe for our faith to sustain.'
The test in that context was the crucial test of the ages to which
Jesus's ministry was the immediate prelude. If we adopt the
rendering of the petition followed in the Series 3 Anglican
Order for Holy Communion, 'Do not bring us to the time of
trial', or the variant proposed by the International Consult-
ation on English Texts, 'Save us from the time of trial', then the
'time of trial' originally intended was one against which the

disciples who were taught to use the petition needed to be forearmed. But the force of the petition would be better expressed by rendering it, 'May our faith stand firm in the time of trial' or 'Save us *in* the time of trial.' Through *that* trial we can no longer pass; the Son of man passed through it as our representative. But the time of trial which will show whether we are truly his followers or not may come upon any Christian at any time. Those who have confidence in their ability to stand such a test may feel no need of the petition. But those who know that their faith is no more reliable than that of Peter and James and John may well pray to be saved from a trial with which their faith cannot cope or, if the trial is inescapable, to be supplied with the heavenly grace necessary to endure it: 'Grant that we may not fail in the test.'

20.

PEARLS BEFORE SWINE

'Do not give dogs what is holy;
and do not throw your pearls before swine,
lest they [the swine] trample them under foot
and [the dogs] turn to attack you' (Matt. 7:6)

The construction of this saying seems to be chiastic. It is the swine that will trample the pearls beneath their feet and the dogs that will turn and bite the hand that fed them, even if it fed them with 'holy' flesh.

The general sense of the saying is clear: objects of value, special privileges, participation in sacred things should not be offered to those who are incapable of appreciating them. Pearls are things of beauty and value to many people – Jesus himself in one of his parables compared the kingdom of God to a 'pearl of great price' (Matt. 13:45–46) – but pigs will despise them because they cannot eat them. Holy flesh – the flesh of sacrificial animals – has a religious value over and above its nutritive value for worshippers who share in a 'peace offering', but pariah dogs will make no difference between it and scraps of offal for which they battle in the street; they will not feel specially grateful to anyone who gives it to them.

But has the saying a more specific application? One could imagine its being quoted by some more restrictive brethren in the Jerusalem church as an argument against presenting the gospel to Gentiles, certainly against receiving them into full Christian fellowship. At a slightly later date it was used as an argument against admitting unbelievers to the Lord's Supper:

thus the *Didache (Teaching of the Twelve Apostles)*, a manual of Syrian Christianity dated around A.D. 100, says: 'Let none eat or drink of your Eucharist except those who have been baptised in the name of the Lord. It was concerning this that the Lord said, "Do not give dogs what is holy." '[1]

It would be anachronistic to read this interpretation back into the ministry of Jesus. It is better to read the saying in the context given it by Matthew (the only Gospel-writer to report it). It comes immediately after the injunction, 'Judge not, that you be not judged' (Matt. 7:1), with two amplifications of that injunction: you will be judged by the standard you apply in the judgment of others (7:2); and you should not try to remove a speck of sawdust from someone else's eye when you have a whole plank in your own (7:3–5). Then comes this saying, which is a further amplification of the principle, or rather a corrective of it: you must not sit in judgment on others and pass censorious sentences on them, but you ought to exercise discrimination. Judgment is an ambiguous word, in English as in Greek: it may mean sitting in judgment on people (or even condemning them), or it may mean exercising a proper discrimination. In the former sense judgment is deprecated; in the latter sense it is recommended. Jesus himself knew that it was useless to impart his message to some people: he had no answer for Herod Antipas when Herod 'questioned him at some length' (Luke 23:9).

With this saying the paragraph on judging in the Sermon on the Mount is concluded; the next paragraph, with its encouragement to ask, seek and knock, turns to another subject.

21.

THE SIN AGAINST THE HOLY SPIRIT

> 'Truly, I say to you, all sins will be forgiven the sons of men, and whatever blasphemies they utter; but whoever blasphemes against the Holy Spirit never has forgiveness, but is guilty of an eternal sin' (Mark 3:28–29)
>
> 'And every one who speaks a word against the Son of man will be forgiven; but he who blasphemes against the Holy Spirit will not be forgiven' (Luke 12:10)

The person who has committed the unpardonable sin figures powerfully in literature. There is, for example, Bunyan's man in the iron cage. There is the Welsh preacher Peter Williams, breaking the silence of night in George Borrow's *Lavengro* with his anguished cry: 'Pechod Ysprydd Glan! O pechod Ysprydd Glan!' ('Oh, the sin against the Holy Spirit!') – which he was persuaded he had committed. Or there is Mr. Paget, in Edmund Gosse's *Father and Son*, who

> had thrown up his cure of souls because he became convinced that he had committed the Sin against the Holy Ghost. ... Mr. Paget was fond of talking, in private and in public, of his dreadful spiritual condition, and he would drop his voice while he spoke of having committed the Unpardonable Sin, with a sort of shuddering exultation, such as people sometimes feel in the possession of a very unusual disease. ... Everybody longed to know what the exact nature had been of that sin against the Holy Ghost

which had deprived Mr. Paget of every glimmer of hope for time or for eternity. It was whispered that even my Father himself was not precisely acquainted with the character of it.[1]

Of course not, because the 'sin' existed only in Mr. Paget's imagination.

In real life there are few more distressing conditions calling for treatment by physicians of the soul than that of people who believe they have committed this sin. When they are offered the gospel assurance of forgiveness for every sin, when they are reminded that 'the blood of Jesus ... cleanses us from all sin' (1 John 1:7), they have a ready answer: there is one sin which forms an exception to this rule, and they have committed that sin; for it, in distinction from all other kinds of sin, there is no forgiveness. Did not our Lord himself say so? And they tend to become impatient when it is pointed out to them (quite truly) that the very fact of their concern over having committed it proves that they have not committed it.

What then did Jesus mean when he spoke in this way? His saying has been preserved in two forms. Luke records it as one of a series of sayings dealing with the Son of man or the Holy Spirit, but Mark gives it a narrative context. (The Marcan and Lucan forms are combined in Matthew 12:31–32.)

According to Mark, scribes or experts in the Jewish law came down from Jerusalem to Galilee to assess the work which, as they heard, Jesus was doing there, and especially his ministry of exorcism – expelling demons from the lives of those who suffered under their domination. (This language indicates a real and sad condition, even if it would commonly be described in different terms today.) The scribes came to a strange conclusion: 'He is possessed by Beelzebul, and by the prince of demons he casts out the demons' (Mark 3:22). (Beelzebul had once been the name of a Canaanite divinity, 'the lord of the high place', but by this time it was used by Jews to denote the ruler of the abyss, the abode of demons.) When Jesus knew of this, he exposed the absurdity of supposing that Satan's power could be overthrown by Satan's aid. Then he went on to charge those who had voiced this absurd conclusion with blaspheming against the Holy Spirit. Why? Because they deliberately ascribed the Holy Spirit's activity to demonic agency.

For every kind of sin, then, for every form of blasphemy or slander, it is implied that forgiveness is available – presumably when the sin is repented of. But what if one were to repent of blasphemy against the Holy Spirit? Is there no forgiveness for the person who repents of this sin?

The answer seems to be that the nature of this sin is such that one does not repent of it, because those who commit it and persist in it do not know that they are sinning. Mark tells his readers why Jesus charged those scribes with blaspheming against the Holy Spirit: it was because 'they had said, "He has an unclean spirit"' (Mark 3:30). Jesus was proclaiming the kingly rule of God, and his bringing relief to soul-sick, demon-possessed mortals was a token that the kingly rule of God was present and active in his ministry. 'If it is by the finger of God that I cast out demons,' he said, 'then the kingdom of God has come upon you' (Luke 11:20; in Matthew 12:28, where these words also appear, 'finger of God' is replaced by 'Spirit of God'). If some people looked at the relief which he was bringing to the bodies and minds of men and women and maintained that he was doing so with the help of their great spiritual oppressor, the prince of the demons, then their eyes were so tightly closed to the light that for them light had become darkness and good had become evil. The light is there for those who will accept it, but if some refuse the light, where else can they hope to receive illumination?

Was Paul sinning against the Holy Spirit in the days when he persecuted Christians and even (according to Acts 26:11) 'tried to make them blaspheme'? Evidently not, because (as it is put in 1 Timothy 1:13) he 'acted ignorantly in unbelief' and therefore received mercy. But if, when he had seen the light on the Damascus road and heard the call of the risen Lord, he had closed his eyes and ears and persevered on his persecuting course, that would have been the 'eternal sin'. But he would not have recognised it as a sin, and so would not have thought of seeking forgiveness for it; he would have gone on thinking that he was doing the work of God, and his conscience would have remained as unperturbed as ever.

Luke, as has been said, gives his form of the saying a different context. He does record the charge that Jesus cast out demons with Beelzebul's aid, but does so in the preceding chapter (Luke 11:14–26) and says nothing there about the sin against the Spirit. His report on Jesus's words about this sin comes in Luke 12:10, immediately after the statement: 'I tell you, every one who acknowledges me before men, the Son of man also will acknowledge before the angels of God; but he who denies me before men will be denied before the angels of God' (Luke 12:8–9). (The second half of this statement is paralleled in Mark 8:38, where it is located in the aftermath to Peter's confession near Caesarea Philippi.) Then, after the words about the sin against the Spirit, Luke quotes the injunction: 'And when they bring you before the synagogues and the rulers and the authorities, do not be anxious how or what you are to answer or what you are to say; for the Holy Spirit will teach you in that very hour what you ought to say' (Luke 12:11–12). This injunction has a parallel in Mark in his version of the Olivet discourse (Mark 13:11); the parallel is taken over in Luke's version of the discourse, where however it is not the Spirit but Jesus who will give his disciples 'a mouth and wisdom' to reply to their inquisitors (Luke 21:15). Matthew has a parallel in his account of the sending out of the twelve apostles: 'What you are to say will be given you in that hour; for it is not you who speak, but the Spirit of your Father speaking through you' (Matt. 10:20).

Luke, then, places the saying about blaspheming the Holy Spirit between a saying about the Spirit's heavenly role as counsel for the defence of those who confess the Son of man (that is, Jesus) and a saying about the Spirit's enabling confessors of Jesus before an earthly tribunal to say the right word at the right time. In this context a different emphasis is given to the matter of blasphemy against the Spirit from that given to it by Mark. It is suggested by Luke that the blaspheming of the Spirit involves a refusal of his powerful help when it is available to save the disciples of Jesus from denying him and so committing apostasy. If so, blasphemy against the Spirit in this context is tantamount to apostasy, the deliberate and decisive repudiation of Jesus as Lord. This is not the only New Testament passage which warns against the irremediable evil of apostasy: another well-known example is Hebrews 6:4–6, where it is said to be impossible to renew apostates to repentance, since they have repudiated the only way of salvation.

But Luke couples with the warning against the unpardonable sin of blasphemy against the Spirit the affirmation of Jesus that there is forgiveness for everyone who speaks a word against the Son of man. On this there are two things to be said.

First, in Jesus's language (Aramaic), the phrase 'the son of man' normally meant 'the man'; only the context could indicate when he intended the phrase to have the special sense which is conveyed by the fuller translation 'the Son of man'. Moreover, in the phrase 'the man' the definite article could, on occasion, have generic force, referring not to a particular human being but to man in general (in English this generic force is best conveyed by using the noun without any article, as in 'Man is born unto trouble, as the sparks fly upward'). So Jesus may have meant, 'To speak against (a) man is pardonable, but to speak against the Spirit is not.'

Secondly, if that is what Jesus meant, he included himself as a man, if not indeed as the representative man (see p. 27). Luke understands him to refer to himself in particular; otherwise he would have said 'everyone who speaks a word against a man' and not (as he does) 'every one who speaks a word against the Son of man'. Why would it be so much more serious to slander the Holy Spirit than to slander the Son of man? Perhaps because the identity of the Son of man was veiled in his humility; people might easily fail to recognise him for who he was. There was nothing in the designation 'the Son of man' in itself to express a claim to authority. The Son of man, at present operating in lowliness and liable to be rejected and ill-treated, might indeed be despised. But if those who had begun to follow him were afraid that, under stress, they might deny him, they were assured that the Spirit's aid was available. If, however, they resisted the Spirit and rejected his aid, then indeed their case would be desperate.

Peter, through fear, denied the Son of man, but he found forgiveness and restoration: his lips had momentarily turned traitor but his heart did not apostatise. His repentance left him wide open to the Spirit's healing grace, and when he was restored, he was able to strengthen others (Luke 22:31–32). Why then, it might be asked, did he not strengthen Ananias and Sapphira when they came to him with part of the proceeds of the sale of their property, pretending that it was the whole amount (see p. 144)? Presumably because, as he said, they had consented to the satanic suggestion that they should 'lie to the Holy Spirit', because they had 'agreed together to tempt the Spirit of the Lord' (Acts 5:3, 9). Thus, in Peter's reckoning, they had sinned beyond the point of no return. How Jesus would have regarded their offence is another question.

In Mark's context, then, the sin against the Holy Spirit involves deliberately shutting one's eyes to the light and consequently calling good evil; in Luke (that is, ultimately, in the sayings collection commonly labelled Q) it is irretrievable apostasy. Probably these are not really two conditions but one – not unlike the condition which Plato described as having the lie in the soul.[2]

22.

NO SIGN

'Why does this generation seek a sign? Truly, I say to you, no sign shall be given to this generation' (Mark 8:12)
'This generation is an evil generation; it seeks a sign, but no sign shall be given to it except the sign of Jonah. For as Jonah became a sign to the men of Nineveh, so will the Son of man be to this generation' (Luke 11:29-30)

Formally, these two sayings appear to contradict each other: 'no sign at all' does not seem to mean the same as 'no sign except the sign of Jonah'. Materially, however, there is little difference in sense between the two, as we shall see when we consider what the sign of Jonah was. In fact, we may be dealing not with two separate sayings but with two variant forms which the same original saying has acquired in the course of transmission. The form preserved by Luke was probably derived from the collection of sayings of Jesus which is conventionally labelled Q. Mark's form reappears in Matthew 16:1-4; the Q form is reproduced in Matthew 12:38-40. Both forms are amplified in Matthew's text and assimilated to one another.

According to Mark, the refusal to give a sign was Jesus's response to some Pharisees who, in the course of debate, asked him to supply 'a sign from heaven'. Jesus spoke and acted with evident authority; what was his authority for speaking and acting as he did? His practice on the sabbath day set at defiance

the traditional interpretation of the sabbath law which had
been built up over the generations; what was his authority for
refusing to accept the 'tradition of the elders'? Whereas the
great prophets of the past had prefaced their proclamation
with 'Thus says the Lord', Jesus was content to set over against
what 'was said to the men of old' his uncompromising 'But *I* say
to you.' What was the basis for this claim to personal
authority?

How can such authority be vindicated? When Moses
approached Pharaoh as the spokesman of the God of Israel
and demanded that his people be allowed to leave Egypt, he
demonstrated the authority by which he spoke in a succession
of signs, such as turning his rod into a serpent and changing
Nile water into blood (Exod. 7:8–24). No doubt Pharaoh was
the sort of person who would be impressed by such signs, but
Moses' enduring right to be recognised as a prophet of the
living God rests on a firmer foundation than such signs. When
Elijah entered the presence of Ahab to denounce his toleration
of Baal-worship in Israel, he confirmed his denunciation with
the announcement of three years' drought (1 Kgs. 17:1). Baal,
the rain-giver, was to be hit in the one place where he could be
hurt – in his reputation. This particular sign was thus highly
relevant to Elijah's message. If Moses and Elijah, then, had
confirmed their authority as messengers of God by signs such
as these, why could not Jesus confirm his authority in a similar
way?

First, what sort of sign would have convinced them?
External signs might have been necessary to convince a
heathen Egyptian or an apostate king of Israel, but why should
they be necessary for custodians and teachers of the law of the
true God? They should have been able to decide without the aid
of signs whether Jesus's teaching was true or not, whether it
was in line or not with the law and the prophets.

Secondly, would the kind of sign they had in mind really
have validated the truth of Jesus's words? Matthew Arnold
remarked, in the course of a nineteenth-century controversy,
that his written statements were unlikely to carry greater
conviction if he demonstrated his ability to turn his pen into a

penwiper.[1] It may be suspected that it was some similarly extraordinary but essentially irrelevant sign that was being asked from Jesus. If, for example, he had thrown himself down in public from the pinnacle of the temple into the Kidron gorge and suffered no harm, that would have done nothing to confirm his teaching about the kingdom of God, even if it would have silenced the demand for a sign.

In the third place, what about the signs he actually performed? Why were they not sufficient to convince his questioners? One Pharisee, indeed, is reported as saying to him, 'Rabbi, we know that you are a teacher come from God; for no one can do these signs that you do, unless God is with him' (John 3:2). Jesus himself affirmed that if it was by the power of God that he relieved those who were demon-possessed, that was a sign of the arrival of the kingdom of God (Luke 11:20; see p. 90). But some of those to whom these words were spoken chose to believe that it was not by the power of God but by the power of the prince of demons that he healed the demon-possessed. If the restoration of bodily and mental health could be dismissed as a work of Satan, no number of healing acts would have established the divine authority by which they were performed.

In his comments on the 'pillar passages' for a scientific life of Jesus, P. W. Schmiedel included Mark 8:12 as the first of four such passages which had a special bearing on the miracles of Jesus. The saying 'No sign shall be given to this generation' was an absolutely authentic one, he maintained, and implied that the miracle stories of the Gospels were secondary constructions. To this it might be said that, while the healing miracles did serve as signs of the kingdom of God to those who had eyes to see, they did not *compel* belief in those who were prejudiced in the opposite direction. The Pharisees mentioned in this incident may have wanted a sign that would compel belief, but can genuine belief ever be compelled? While the miracles served as signs, they were not performed in order to be signs. They were as much part and parcel of Jesus's ministry as was his preaching – not, as it has been put, seals affixed to the document to certify its genuineness but an integral element in the very text of the document.[2] No sign would be given which was not already available in the ministry itself; to ask for more was a mark of unbelief.

What, now, of the sign of Jonah? Jonah, it is said, was 'a sign to the men of Nineveh'. How? By his one-sentence message of judgment. That was all the 'sign' that the people of Nineveh had; it was sufficient to move them to belief and repentance. Schmiedel illustrates that there is no real contradiction between 'no sign' absolutely and 'no sign except the sign of Jonah' by the analogy of an aggressor who invades a neighbouring country without provocation. When asked what justification he can give for his action, he replies, 'I shall give you no other justification than that which my sword gives' – which is as much as to say 'no justification'. As Jonah's ministry in Nineveh was sign enough, so Jesus's ministry in Palestine is sign enough. No other sign would be given.

In the Q collection the refusal to give any sign but the sign of Jonah was followed by a comparison between the people to whom Jesus ministered and those to whom Jonah preached. Jesus's hearers shared the rich heritage of divine worship and revelation which had been enjoyed over the centuries by the people of Israel; Jonah preached to pagans. Yet Jonah's hearers made a swift and positive response to his message; the reaction on the part of the majority of Jesus's hearers was quite different. Therefore, he said, 'The men of Nineveh will arise at the judgment with this generation and condemn it; for they repented at the preaching of Jonah, and behold, something greater than Jonah is here' (Matt. 12:41; Luke 11:32). The 'something greater' was Jesus's proclamation of the kingdom of God, which was more important and far-reaching than Jonah and his preaching. Yet Jonah and his preaching were enough to bring the people of Nineveh to repentance; Jesus's proclamation of the kingdom made no such large-scale impact on his generation. On the day of judgment, therefore, the people of Nineveh would compare very favourably with the Galileans to whom Jesus preached; indeed, they would serve as tacit, if not as vocal, witnesses against them. Whether these words of Jesus were spoken on the same occasion as the saying about the sign or on another occasion, their relevance to it is unmistakable.

Matthew, for his part, adds a further analogy between Jonah's situation and that of Jesus: 'As Jonah was three days and three nights in the belly of the whale, so will the Son of man be three days and three nights in the heart of the earth' (Matt. 12:40). This is commonly supposed to be a later insertion among the Jonah sayings. T. W. Manson, however, suggests that no one after the resurrection of Jesus, which by common Christian consent took place on 'the third day', would have represented him as being buried for a much longer period[3]. This would point to a life-setting for the Matthaean saying before Jesus's death and resurrection. In any case, it would be unwise to press 'three days and three nights' to mean 72 hours, neither more nor less. Jonah's experience in the Mediterranean was not a sign to the people of Nineveh, any more than Jesus's resurrection on Easter Day after his entombment on Good Friday was a public spectacle. In Matthew 12:40 we simply have an analogy traced between two servants of God, who were both brought up by God 'from the Pit' (Jonah 2:6; cf. Ps. 16:10, quoted with reference to Jesus in Acts 2:27; 13:35).

23.

SEEING AND NOT PERCEIVING

'To you has been given the secret of the kingdom of God, but for those outside everything is in parables; so that they may indeed see but not perceive, and may indeed hear but not understand; lest they should turn again, and be forgiven' (Mark 4:11–12)

This saying comes in Mark's record between the parable of the sower (or parable of the four soils, as some prefer to call it) and the explanation of that parable. The parable, the explanation, and the saying quoted above are all ascribed to Jesus himself. But if the saying means what it seems to mean, then Jesus tells his disciples that the purpose of his use of parables is that his hearers in general (those who are not his followers) may hear him but not understand him; and it is difficult to believe that this was so.

Matthew alters the sense by using the conjunction 'because' instead of 'so that': 'This is why I speak to them in parables, because seeing they do not see, and hearing they do not hear, nor do they understand' (Matt. 13:13). That is to say, because the general public was slow to grasp the sense of Jesus's teaching, he embodied it in parables to make it more immediately intelligible. The hardness of the saying is thus mitigated; it is readily accepted that:

Truth embodied in a tale
Shall enter in at lowly doors.[1]

Luke 8:10 follows Mark's construction, with some abbreviation.

But what is the point of Mark's construction? One suggestion is that the saying was entirely Mark's creation. The parable, it is said, was told by Jesus; the explanation received its shape in the primitive Church, but the hard saying is Mark's own contribution: it expresses his view (or the view of the school of thought to which he belonged) about the purpose of Jesus's parables. But is it out of the question that the saying represents something spoken by Jesus himself?

It is plain that the saying is an adaptation of an Old Testament text, Isaiah 6:9–10. When Isaiah received his call to the prophetic ministry, in the well-known vision that he saw in the temple 'in the year that King Uzziah died', the voice of God said to him, 'Go, and say to this people: "Hear and hear, but do not understand; see and see, but do not perceive." Make the heart of this people fat, and their ears heavy, and shut their eyes; lest they see with their eyes, and hear with their ears, and understand with their hearts, and turn and be healed.'

Should this commission be pressed to mean that Isaiah was ordered to go and tell the people to pay no heed to what they heard him say? Was it his prescribed duty to prevent them from hearing and understanding his message, and thus make it impossible for them to repent and so escape the destruction that would otherwise overtake them? No indeed; if that impression is given, it is simply due to the Hebrew tendency to express a consequence as though it were a purpose. Isaiah volunteers to be God's messenger to his people, and God takes him at his word, but says to him in effect, 'Go and deliver my message, but don't expect them to pay any attention to it. The effect of your preaching will be their persistent refusal to accept what you say, to the point where they will have rendered themselves incapable of accepting it.' In the event, this is exactly what Isaiah was to experience for the next forty years.

Isaiah's experience was reproduced in Jesus's ministry. For all the enthusiasm which greeted his ministry in its earlier phase, he had later on to lament the unbelief with which he met in the very places where most of his mighty works had been done. He might well have applied the words of Isaiah 6:9-10 to the effect (not, of course, to the purpose) of his own ministry. Certainly this text became one of the commonest Old Testament 'testimonies' in the early Church on the subject of Jewish resistance to the gospel. Apart from the allusion to it in the context of the parable of the sower in all three synoptic Gospels, it is quoted in John 12:40 at the end of Jesus's Jerusalem ministry and in Acts 28:26-27 at Paul's meeting with the Jewish leaders in Rome, while there is an echo of it in Romans 11:8. Its pervasiveness in this sense could well be due to Jesus's application of it to his own experience. 'As in its original setting in the Book of Isaiah, so here, it is most naturally taken as an arresting, hyperbolical, oriental way of saying, "Alas! many will be obdurate."'[2]

At the end of the Isaiah quotation the verb used is 'be healed'. It is so in the Hebrew text and it is so in the Greek version (the Septuagint). But in the corresponding position in Mark 4:12 the verb is 'be forgiven'. This might be set down as a free paraphrase on the evangelist's part, were it not that the Aramaic Targum on the Prophets has 'be forgiven'. The date of the written Targum on the Prophets is considerably later than the date of Mark, but behind the written Targum lies an oral tradition: the Aramaic paraphrase of the Hebrew lesson was originally given in the synagogue by word of mouth. Perhaps, then, 'be forgiven' is due not to Mark but to Jesus: speaking in Aramaic, he alluded to the Aramaic wording of the Isaiah passage.

Recognising this, T. W. Manson went on to make a further suggestion.[3] If Jesus had the Aramaic version of the text in mind, then it is relevant to consider that in Aramaic one and the same form does duty for 'so that' and 'who', while the expression for 'lest' may also mean 'perhaps'. The meaning of Jesus's saying would then be: 'For those outside everything is in parables, (for those, namely) who see indeed but do not perceive, who hear indeed but do not understand; perhaps they may turn again and be forgiven'.

This certainly removes most of the hardness from the saying, making it mean that Jesus imparted the 'mystery' of the kingdom of God to the disciples but spoke in parables to those outside their circle in hope that they would grasp sufficient of his teaching to repent and receive forgiveness. But if this is what the saying meant, Mark (or his source of information) has misunderstood it and made it hard.

If we remember that in the idiom of Jesus and his contemporaries a result might be expressed as though it were a purpose, the saying remains hard, but not intolerably hard. It is helpful also to realise that in Hebrew and Aramaic the word for 'parable' might also mean 'riddle'.

Jesus proclaimed the kingdom of God and made plain the far-reaching implications of its arrival. This was a 'mystery' in the sense that it had not been disclosed in this form before: Jesus revealed it in his ministry. Among his hearers there were some whose minds were open to his teaching; they grasped its meaning and appreciated the point of his parables. There were others whose minds were closed. Even if at first they thought that he was the teacher and leader for whom they had been waiting, they soon changed their minds. His parables, luminous to those who had eyes to see and ears to hear, were but riddles to them. They could not take his message in, and so they could not profit by it. The more he spoke and acted among them, the less responsive they became. And they were in the majority. Only a few, relatively speaking, embraced the good news of the kingdom, but for their sake it was worthwhile making it known.

If the saying is understood in this sense, its relevance to the context, immediately after the parable of the sower, should be clear. The sower scattered the good seed broadcast, but only a quarter of it yielded a crop, because of the poor soil on which the rest of it fell – the hard-beaten path, the thorn-infested ground, the shallow skin of earth on top of the rock. But the harvest that sprang up from the good and fertile ground meant that the labour of sowing was by no means in vain – quite the contrary. The gain derived from those 'who hear the word and accept it' more than outweighs the loss incurred through those who turn away.

24.

GO NOWHERE AMONG THE GENTILES

'Go nowhere among the Gentiles, and enter no town of the Samaritans, but go rather to the lost sheep of the house of Israel' (Matt. 10:5-6)

These words occur in Matthew's account of Jesus's sending out the twelve apostles two by two at a fairly early stage in his Galilean ministry, in order that the proclamation of the kingdom of God might be carried on more extensiveiy and more quickly than if he had done it by himself alone. The message they were to preach was the same as he preached: 'The kingdom of heaven is at hand.' The works of healing that were to accompany their preaching were of the same kind as accompanied his.

Mark (6:7-13) and Luke (9:1-6) also report the sending out of the twelve, but more briefly than Matthew does. Matthew is the only evangelist to include these 'exclusive' words in his account. 'The lost sheep of the house of Israel' is an expression peculiar to his Gospel (although it is not dissimilar to 'sheep without a shepherd' in Mark 6:34); it occurs again in his account of the healing of the Canaanite woman's daughter (Matt. 15:24).

Since Matthew is the only evangelist to report these words, it might be argued that they were not originally spoken by Jesus, but were ascribed to him by the evangelist or his source. We cannot make Matthew responsible for inventing them: there is no reason to think that Matthew had an anti-Gentile bias or entertained a particularist view of the gospel. At the beginning of his record he brings the Gentiles in by telling how the wise men came from the east to pay homage to the infant king of the Jews – the occasion traditionally referred to as the 'epiphany' or 'manifestation' of Christ to the Gentiles. In the course of his report of Jesus's teaching he quotes him as saying that, before the end comes, 'this gospel of the kingdom will be preached throughout all the world, as a testimony to all nations' (Matt. 24:14). At the end of the book (Matt. 28:19) he tells how the risen Christ commissioned the apostles to 'go ... and make disciples of all nations' (that is, among all the Gentiles). And in the course of his record he tells of Jesus's praise for the Roman centurion of Capernaum, in whom he found greater faith than he had found in any Israelite (Luke 7:2–10), and of his following assertion that 'many will come from east and west and sit at table with Abraham, Isaac and Jacob in the kingdom of heaven', while some of the descendants of Abraham, Isaac and Jacob would find themselves excluded from the feast (Matt. 8:5–13; cf. Luke 13:28–29; see p. 200.) Those last words would certainly be a hard saying for Jewish hearers, just as hard as 'Go nowhere among the Gentiles' might be for Gentile readers.

Matthew probably did derive some of the material peculiar to his Gospel from a source marked by a Jewish emphasis – perhaps a compilation of sayings of Jesus preserved by a rather strict Jewish-Christian community. 'Go nowhere among the Gentiles' may well have been found in this source.[1] But the source in question probably selected those sayings of Jesus which chimed in with its own outlook; that is no argument against their genuineness.

When Jesus sent out the twelve, the time at their disposal was short, and it was necessary to concentrate on the people who had been specially prepared for the message of the kingdom. Even if the twelve did confine themselves to the 'lost sheep of the house of Israel', they would not have time to cover all of these. This had sometimes been thought to be the point of the words: 'you will not have gone through all the towns of Israel, before the Son of man comes' (Matt. 10:23), cryptic words which must be considered by themselves – see p. 107.

Moreover, it is taught in the prophetic writings of the Old Testament, and nowhere more clearly than in Isaiah 40–55, that when Israel grasps the true knowledge of God, it will be her privilege to share that knowledge with other nations. Nearly thirty years later, Paul, apostle to the Gentiles though he was, lays down the order of gospel presentation as being 'to the Jew first and also to the Greek' (Rom. 1:16) – the 'Greek' here standing for the Gentile. This statement of primitive evangelistic policy was evidently founded on Jesus's own practice. Even so, there are hints here and there in the synoptic Gospels that the Gentiles' interests were not forgotten. The incident of the Roman centurion of Capernaum has been mentioned; the healing of the Canaanite woman's daughter will receive separate treatment – see p. 110. Such occasions, isolated and exceptional as they were during Jesus's ministry, foreshadowed the mission to the Gentiles which was launched a few years after his death. The Fourth Gospel emphasises this by relating an incident which took place in Jerusalem during Holy Week, only two or three days before Jesus's arrest and crucifixion. Some Greeks who were visiting the city approached one of the disciples and asked for an interview with Jesus. His reply, when he was told of their request, was in effect 'Not yet, but after my death' – 'when I am lifted up from the earth, I will draw all men to myself', all without distinction, Gentiles and Jews alike (John 12:20–32). That is exactly what happened.

The ban on entering any town of the Samaritans is to be understood in the same way. Samaritans were not Jews, but neither were they Gentiles. Jesus did not share his people's anti-Samaritan bias (although the evidence for this is supplied by Luke and John, not by Matthew), and after his death and resurrection his message of salvation was effectively presented to Samaritans even before it was presented to Gentiles (Acts 8:5–25).

25

YOU WILL NOT HAVE GONE THROUGH ALL THE TOWNS OF ISRAEL

*'When they persecute you in one town, flee to the next;
for truly, I say to you, you will not have gone through
all the towns of Israel, before the Son of man comes'*
(Matt. 10:23)

This saying, found in Matthew's Gospel only, comes at the end of Jesus's commission to the twelve apostles when he sent them out two by two. It was brought to public attention early in the twentieth century when the great Albert Schweitzer made it the foundation of his interpretation of the ministry of Jesus. Jesus, he believed, expected the kingdom of God to dawn with power and glory at harvest time that year, before the twelve had completed their mission. 'He tells them in plain words ... that He does not expect to see them back in the present age.'[1] Jesus would be supernaturally revealed as the Son of man, in a manner involving his own transformation, as well as the transformation of his followers, into a state of being suited to the conditions of the resurrection age. But the new age did not come in; the twelve returned from their mission. Jesus then tried to force its arrival. He 'lays hold of the wheel of the world to set it moving on that last revolution which is to bring all ordinary history to a close. It refuses to turn, and He throws Himself upon it. Then it does turn; and crushes Him.'[2] Yet in the hour of his failure he released a liberating power in the world which is beyond description.

The teaching of the Sermon on the Mount and related passages in the Gospels was understood by Dr. Schweitzer to be an 'interim ethic' to guide the lives of Jesus's disciples in the short interval before the manifestation of the Son of man in power and glory. When, on Dr. Schweitzer's reading of the evidence, the hope of that manifestation was disappointed, what happened to the interim ethic? Logically, it should have been forgotten when its basis was removed. Actually, the interim ethic survived in its own right, as is magnificently evident from Dr. Schweitzer's own career. It was the driving force behind his life of service to others in West Africa. What, on his understanding, was but the prologue to the expected drama 'has become the whole drama . . . the ministry of Jesus is not a prelude to the Kingdom of God: it *is* the Kingdom of God.'[3]

The commission to the twelve, as given in Matthew 10:5-23, has two parts, each with its own perspective. The first part (verses 5-15) deals with the immediate situation, within the context of Jesus's own Galilean ministry. The second part (verses 16-23) envisages a later period, when the apostles will be engaged in a wider ministry – the kind of ministry in which in fact they were engaged in the period *following* the resurrection of Jesus and the coming of the Spirit. Think of the warning: 'Beware of men; for they will deliver you up to councils, and flog you in their synagogues, and you will be dragged before governors and kings for my sake, to bear testimony before them and the Gentiles' (Matt. 10:17-18). This reference to the Gentiles presents a contrast with the reference to them in verse 5, where they are excluded from the scope of the earlier preaching tour. The warning just quoted has a close parallel in Mark 13:9-10, where the situation is that leading up to the destruction of Jerusalem in A.D. 70. And in both places the warning is followed by an assurance that, when the disciples are put on trial and required to bear witness to their faith, the Holy Spirit will put the right words into their mouths. It is this second part of the commission in Matthew 10 that is rounded off with the saying of verse 23: 'You will not have gone through all the towns of Israel, before the Son of man comes.'

What, then, does the saying mean in *this* context? It means, simply, that the evangelisation of Israel will not be completed before the end of the present age, which comes with the advent of the Son of man. The parallel passage in Mark has a similar statement, which however takes more explicit account of Gentile as well as Jewish evangelisation: before the end-time, 'the gospel must first be preached to all the nations' (Mark 13:10). (This statement is reproduced in slightly amplified form in Matthew 24:14: 'This gospel of the kingdom will be preached throughout the whole world, as a testimony to all the nations; and then the end will come'.) Paul, from his own perspective, expresses much the same hope when he foresees the salvation of 'all Israel', the sequel to the ingathering of the full tale of Gentile believers, being consummated at the time when 'the Deliverer will come from Zion' (Rom. 11:25–27).

The wording of Matthew 10:23 is earlier in its reference than that of the other passages just mentioned: here witness-bearing to the Gentiles receives a brief mention, but all the emphasis lies on the mission to the Jews. This mission, as we know from Galatians 2:6–9, was taken seriously by the leaders of the Jerusalem Church in the early apostolic age, and they carried it out with some sense of urgency. For anything they knew to the contrary, the Son of man might come within their own generation. We must not allow our understanding of their perspective to be influenced by our own very different perspective. We know that their mission, in the form in which they pursued it, was brought to an end by the Judaean rebellion against Rome in A.D. 66, but it would be unwise to say that *that*, with the fall of Jerusalem four years later, was the coming of the Son of man of which Jesus spoke.

26.

LET THE CHILDREN FIRST BE FED

'Let the children first be fed, for it is not right to take the children's bread and throw it to the dogs' (Mark 7:27)

This was Jesus's response to the plea of a Gentile woman that he would cure her demon-possessed daughter. The woman was a Syrophoenician according to Mark, a Canaanite according to Matthew, who also records the incident (Matt. 15:21–28). The incident took place during a brief visit paid by Jesus to the territory of Tyre and Sidon, north of Galilee.

The saying was a hard one in the first instance to the woman, yet not so hard that it put her off: if Jesus's healing ministry was for Jewish children and not for Gentile dogs, yet she reminded him that the dogs commonly get what the children leave over, and that was what she was asking him to give her and her daughter. To the modern reader it is hard because it seems so inconsistent with the character of Jesus. Its hardness is put in blunt terms by one writer: 'Long familiarity with this story, together with the traditional picture of the gentleness of Jesus, tends to obscure the shocking intolerance of the saying.'[1]

Jesus's Palestinian ministry was directed to the Jewish people: Matthew, in his account of the present incident, represents him as saying to the woman, 'I was sent only to the lost sheep of the house of Israel' (Matt. 15:24). There are suggestions here and there in the record of the ministry that, as a sequel to it, blessing would be available for Gentiles too, but very few instances of direct blessing to Gentiles appear within the context of the ministry itself.

Why did the woman not take offence at such an unpromising reply to her request? One obvious reason was that she was determined to get what she wanted for her daughter. In addition, what if there was a twinkle in his eye as he spoke, as much as to say, 'You know what we Jews are supposed to think of you Gentiles; do you think it is right for you to come and ask for a share in the healing which I have come to impart to Jews?' The written record can preserve the spoken words; it cannot convey the tone of voice in which they were said. Maybe the tone of voice encouraged the woman to persevere.

Again, what are we to say of the term 'dogs'? That is a term of abuse, if ever there was one. The pariah dog was not an estimable animal in Near Eastern culture then, any more than he is today. But it is not the pariah dogs that are intended here, like those at the door of the rich man in the parable, whose attentions added to Lazarus's afflictions. It is the dogs beneath the table. That in itself might suggest that they are household pets, the children's playmates; and this is confirmed by the fact that the word for 'dogs' used by both Jesus and the woman is a diminutive. Since the woman is said by Mark to have been a Greek (i.e. one who spoke Greek), the Greek diminutive used by Mark may have been the word actually used in the conversation.

The woman was quick-witted enough to deduce from Jesus's words the kind of reply to him that would win the granting of her request: 'Sir, even the little dogs under the table eat the children's left-overs!' The word 'faith' is not mentioned in Mark's account of the incident (as it is mentioned in Matthew 15:28), but the woman's reply expresses just the kind of faith that Jesus so greatly appreciated and that never failed to receive what it asked from him. Jesus was aware of a greater rapport with him on her part than he too often found among his own people. Her daughter was healed immediately, and healed, as in the other instance of Gentile faith in the synoptic Gospels (that of the Capernaum centurion and his sick servant – see p. 105), not by direct contact but at a distance.

27.

WHO IS GREATER THAN JOHN THE BAPTIST?

'I tell you, among those born of women none is greater than John; yet he who is least in the kingdom of God is greater than he' (Luke 7:28; cf. Matt. 11:11)

With minor variations, this saying is reproduced by both Matthew and Luke in the same context. Matthew's wording is slightly fuller and, as usual, he has 'kingdom of heaven' where his parallel has 'kingdom of God'. (The two expressions are completely synonymous; then as now there were some who used 'heaven' as a substitute for the name of God.)

The saying is paradoxical: if John was not surpassed in greatness by any human being, how could anyone be greater than he? The paradox was certainly deliberate: we may wonder if any of Jesus's hearers grasped the point more readily than we do today.

In both Gospels the saying comes in the sequel to the account of the deputation of disciples which John, who was then imprisoned by Herod Antipas, tetrarch of Galilee and Perea, sent to Jesus. In his preaching in the lower Jordan valley John had called on his hearers to amend their ways in preparation for the Coming One, who would carry out a judgment symbolised by wind and fire (Luke 3:17; Matt. 3:12; see p. 123). Judgment involved the separation of the good from the worthless, the wheat from the chaff. The chaff, blown away by the wind, would be swept up and thrown into the fire.

After the baptism of Jesus, John recognised him as the

Coming One of whom he spoke, but now he was not so sure. Jesus had begun his own ministry, but from the reports of it which reached John in prison, it bore little resemblance to the ministry of judgment which John had foretold for the Coming One. Hence he sent his disciples to ask Jesus, 'Are you the Coming One, or must we look for someone else?'

Jesus might have told the messengers to go back and say to John that the answer to his question was, 'Yes, I am the Coming One; there is no need to look for anyone else.' But that would not have been very satisfactory. John might have said, 'Ah! but he might be mistaken himself.' Instead, Jesus kept the messengers with him for some time, and they heard and saw what was actually happening in his ministry. Then, when he judged that they had heard and seen enough for his purpose, he sent them back to tell John all about it – how the blind had their sight restored, the lame were walking, the deaf were enabled to hear and so forth, and how the good news was being proclaimed to the poor. 'Tell him this too,' he added: 'Blessed is the man who does not feel that I have let him down' (Matt. 11:2–6; Luke 7:19–23).

Jesus knew what John would make of his disciples' report. Jesus was doing the very things which, according to the prophets, would mark the inbreaking of the new age: 'Then the eyes of the blind shall be opened, and the ears of the deaf unstopped; then shall the lame man leap like a hart, and the tongue of the dumb sing for joy' (Isa. 35:5–6). Above all, he was actively fulfilling, and indeed embodying, the prophetic word which said, 'The Spirit of the Lord God is upon me, because the Lord has anointed me to bring good tidings to the poor ...' (Isa. 61:1). This should convince John that Jesus was indeed the Coming One: John had not been mistaken about him and need not feel that Jesus was letting him down by not doing the kind of thing John had said he would do.

When the messengers had departed, Jesus began to speak to the crowd about John in terms of unqualified commendation. John was nobody's yes-man, no weather-vane; he stood four-square to every wind that blew and declared the message of God without fear or favour, to peasant and prince. And when

Jesus asked them if they went out to the wilderness to see 'a man clothed in soft raiment', they must have laughed, as they remembered John's rough coat of camel's hair. No, said Jesus, for people who wear fine clothes and eat more luxurious food than John's diet of locusts and wild honey you have to go to royal courts – and John was not at the royal court but in the royal jail. John was a prophet, as most people thought; yes, said Jesus, and more than a prophet; he was God's special messenger sent to prepare his way, foretold in Malachi 3:1; he was, in fact, unsurpassed by any other. 'Among those born of women none is greater than John.' John spoke of the Coming One as 'he who is mightier than I', but here is the Coming One, himself born of a woman, paying a remarkable tribute to John. Then why did he add, 'yet he who is least in the kingdom of God is greater than he'?

I think we can ignore the suggestion that 'the least in the kingdom of God' was a reference to Jesus himself. 'The least in the kingdom of God' is the most insignificant person who enjoys the blessings of the new age of salvation which Jesus was bringing in. John was like Moses, who viewed the promised land from the top of Mount Pisgah, but did not enter it; he was the last of the heroes of Hebrews 11 who, 'though well attested by their faith, did not receive what was promised'. It is not in moral stature or devotion or service, but in privilege, that those who are least in the kingdom of God are greater than John – greater not for what they do for God (in this John was unsurpassed) but for what God does for them. On another occasion Jesus congratulated his disciples because they lived to see and hear what many prophets and kings had longed in vain to see and hear (Luke 10:23–24). It was not because of any superior merit of theirs that the disciples enjoyed these blessings: it was because they lived at the time when Jesus came and were called by him to share the life and service of the kingdom of God. Even to be his herald and forerunner, as John was, was not such a great privilege as to participate in the ministry of the Coming One, to be heirs of the kingdom which John, as the last of the prophets of old, foresaw and foretold.

28.

VIOLENCE AND THE KINGDOM

'From the days of John the Baptist until now the kingdom of heaven has suffered violence, and men of violence take it by force' (Matt. 11:12)
   'The law and the prophets were until John; since then the good news of the kingdom of God is preached, and every one enters it violently' (Luke 16:16)

Matthew and Luke appear to present us here with two versions of one and the same original saying. We have to try to determine what each of the two versions means in the context in which either evangelist has placed it; then, if possible, we have to determine what the original saying meant in the context of Jesus's ministry.

Both versions agree on this: the ministry of John the Baptist was an epoch marking the end of one age and the approach of a new. 'All the prophets and the law prophesied until John' (Matt. 11:13). John himself belonged rather to the old age than to the new. He is viewed as being the last and greatest of the 'goodly fellowship of the prophets'; while he was the herald of the new order he did not actually participate in it. When his public ministry was forcibly ended by his imprisonment, that was the signal for Jesus to embark on *his* ministry in Galilee, with the proclamation that the kingdom of God had drawn near.

'Since then', says Jesus in Luke's version of his words, 'the good news of the kingdom of God is preached.' That was a statement of fact, which his hearers must have recognised. But in what sense does everyone enter it violently?

Luke includes his version in a series of sayings inserted between the story of the dishonest steward and the story of the rich man and Lazarus and linked together by the general theme of law. 'Everyone forces his way in', says the NEB; the Good News Bible has the same wording. This might suggest something like a universal gate-crashing, which does not tally too well with some other sayings of Jesus on the relative fewness of those who enter the kingdom, such as 'Strive to enter by the narrow door; for many, I tell you, will seek to enter and will not be able' (Luke 13:24; cf. Matt. 7:13–14). But perhaps the meaning is, 'Everyone who enters must force his way in', which implies the same kind of determined and vigorous action as 'Strive to enter'. So far as the Lucan version of the saying goes, this could well be its meaning. It was no doubt this interpretation of it that moved an eighteenth-century hymn-writer to say, in language which probably sounded less strange in his contemporaries' ears than it does in ours:

> O may thy mighty word
> Inspire each feeble worm
> To rush into thy kingdom, Lord,
> And take it as by storm!

But Matthew's version now demands our attention. Where Luke says 'The good news of the kingdom of God is preached', Matthew says 'The kingdom of heaven has been suffering violence'. But there is an ambiguity in the particular form of the Greek verb in this clause: it may have passive force, meaning 'has been treated with violence' or 'has been suffering violence', or it may have intransitive force, meaning 'has been acting violently' or 'has been forcing its way in'. It could be said in favour of this last interpretation that in the ministry of Jesus the kingdom of heaven was on the march, taking the field against the forces of evil that held the souls and bodies of men and women in bondage. The mighty works that were an essential part of his ministry were the 'powers of the age to come' invading the present age and establishing a beach-head on its territory which was destined to expand until nothing of the old order was left.

If the passive force of the verb be preferred, then Jesus says that from the time of John the Baptist the kingdom of heaven has been violently attacked. This meaning too could fit the setting of the words. Matthew records them among several of Jesus's sayings about John (including the description of him as unsurpassed among those born of women) which he appends to the incident of John's messengers who were sent to question Jesus. It could be said that the imprisonment of John the Baptist (with his ensuing execution) was one instance of a violent attack on the kingdom of heaven by forces opposed to it – whether one thinks of human forces or demonic forces using men as their instruments. Further attacks were to be experienced until they reached their climax in the arrest and crucifixion of Jesus himself. The same meaning could be attached to the following clause: 'and men of violence take it by force' or 'men of violence seize it'. In that case, the two clauses say very much the same thing.

But the 'men of violence' need not be those who violently attacked the kingdom which Jesus proclaimed. There were other 'men of violence' around at the time – those who came later to be known as the party of the Zealots. They were passionately devoted to the bringing in of the kingdom of God, but their methods were clean contrary to those which Jesus practised and recommended. The kingdom of God, as they understood it, was a new order in which the Jewish people would live in freedom from Gentile rule, subject to no king but the God of their fathers. This new order could be introduced only by the forcible expulsion of the occupying Roman power from Judaea. Many of Jesus's hearers could remember the revolt of one such 'man of violence', Judas the Galilean, in A.D. 6. That revolt was crushed by the Romans, but the spirit which inspired it lived on. It could be said that men of this outlook were trying to take the kingdom of God by force, and on the whole it seems most probable that Jesus was referring to them.

Matthew's wording, then, seems to mean that, despite the

setback which the cause of God might have seemed to suffer by the imprisonment of John the Baptist, his kingdom has in reality been advancing irresistibly ever since. Men of violence may attempt to speed its progress by armed force, but that is not the way in which its triumph will be assured.

When Luke's account and Matthew's are compared, it appears that Matthew's wording is more relevant to the immediate circumstances of Jesus's ministry, while Luke's wording generalises the application of the saying, showing how its principle continued to work itself out in the world-wide proclamation and progress of the gospel. The good news was still being made known, and it still called for courage and resolution to enter the kingdom of God.

29.

HATING ONE'S PARENTS

'If any one comes to me and does not hate his own father and mother and wife and children and brothers and sisters, yes, and even his own life, he cannot be my disciple' (Luke 14:26)

This is a hard saying in more senses than one: it is hard to accept and it is hard to reconcile it with the general teaching of Jesus. The attitude which it seems to recommend goes against the grain of nature, and it also goes against the law of love to one's neighbour which Jesus emphasised and radicalised. If the meaning of 'neighbour' must be extended so as to include one's enemy, it must not be restricted so as to exclude one's nearest and dearest.

What does it mean, then? It means that, just as property can come between us and the kingdom of God (see p. 174), so can family ties. The interests of God's kingdom must be paramount with the followers of Jesus, and everything else must take second place to them, even family ties. We tend to agree that there is something sordid about the attitude which gives priority to money-making over the nobler and more humane issues of life. But a proper care for one's family is one of those nobler and more humane issues. Jesus himself censured those theologians who argued that people who had vowed to give God a sum of money which they later discovered could have been used to help their parents in need were not free to divert the money from the religious purposes to which it had been vowed in order to meet a parental need. This, he said, was a violation of the commandment to honour one's father and mother (Mark 7:9–13).

Nevertheless, a man or woman might be so bound up by family ties as to have no time or interest for matters of even greater moment, and there could be no matter of greater moment than the kingdom of God. The husband and father was normally the head of the household, and he might look on his family as an extension of his own personality to the point where love for his family was little more than an extended form of self-love. Jesus strongly deprecated such an inward-looking attitude and used the strongest terms to express his disapproval of it. If 'hating' one's relatives is felt to be a shocking idea, it was meant to be shocking, to shock the hearers into a sense of the imperious demands of the kingdom of God. We know that in biblical idiom to hate can mean to love less. When, for example, regulations are laid down in the Old Testament law for a man who has two wives, 'one beloved and the other hated' (Deut. 21:15), it is not necessary to suppose that he positively hates the latter wife; all that need be meant is that he loves her less than the other and must be prevented from showing favouritism to the other's son when he allocates his property among his heirs. The RSV indicates that positive hatred is not intended by speaking of the one wife as 'the loved' and the other as 'the disliked', but the Hebrew word used is that which regularly means 'hated', and it is so rendered in the AV.

That hating in this saying of Jesus means loving less is shown by the parallel saying in Matthew 10:37: 'He who loves father or mother more than me is not worthy of me; and he who loves son or daughter more than me is not worthy of me.' In Matthew's Gospel these words are followed by the saying about taking up the cross and following Jesus (see p. 150): the implication of this sequence is that giving one's family second place to the kingdom of God is one way of taking up the cross.

We can perhaps understand more easily the action of those who choose a celibate life to devote themselves more unreservedly to the service of God, those who, as Jesus said on another occasion, 'have made themselves eunuchs for the sake of the kingdom of heaven' (Matt. 19:12; see p. 63). But the saying with which we are at present concerned refers to those who are already married and have children, not to speak of dependent parents. That Jesus's followers included some who had dependents like these and had left them to follow him is plain from his own words: 'There is no one who has left house or brothers or sisters or mother or father or children or lands, for my sake and for the gospel, ... who will not receive a hundredfold now in this time, ... and in the age to come eternal life' (Mark 10:29–30). Might this not involve the abandonment of natural responsibilities? Who, for example, looked after Peter's family when he took to the road as a disciple of Jesus? We are not told. Clearly his wife survived the experience, and her affections apparently survived it also, for twenty-five years later he was accustomed to take her along with him on his missionary journeys (1 Cor. 9:5).

Later in the New Testament period, when family life was acknowledged as the norm for Christians, it is laid down that, 'If any one does not provide for his relatives, and especially for his own family, he has disowned the faith and is worse than an unbeliever' (1 Tim. 5:8). There is no evidence in the Gospels that this conflicts with the teaching of Jesus. But this needed no emphasising from him: it is natural for men and women to make what provision they can for their nearest and dearest. Jesus's emphasis lay rather on the necessity of treating the kingdom of God as nearer and dearer still. Because of the natural resistance on the part of his hearers to accepting this necessity with literal seriousness, he insisted on it in the most arresting and challenging language at his command.

30

CASTING FIRE ON EARTH

'I came to cast fire upon the earth; and would that it were already kindled!' (Luke 12:49)

This saying is hard in the sense of being difficult to understand, mainly because it is not obviously related to the context in which it appears. It may be thought probable that it is somehow connected with the saying immediately following (see p. 125), about the baptism which Jesus had to undergo before current restraints were removed, but this cannot be taken for granted: each of the two sayings must first be examined by itself.

It is natural to link the 'fire' in this saying with the 'fire' mentioned in John the Baptist's description of the work to be accomplished by the one whose way he was preparing: 'He who is mightier than I is coming, the thong of whose sandals I am not worthy to untie; he will baptize you with the Holy Spirit and with fire' (Luke 3:16). The fire is closely associated here with the Holy Spirit. A shorter form of John's words is found in Mark 1:8; there, however, there is no mention of fire: 'He will baptise you with the Holy Spirit'. Matthew, like Luke, adds the words 'and with fire' (Matt. 3:11), and both Matthew and Luke go on to report further words of John about the Coming One: 'His winnowing fork is in his hand, and he will clear his threshing floor and gather his wheat into the granary, but the chaff he will burn with unquenchable fire' (Matt. 3:12; Luke 3:17). It is worth bearing in mind that the same word is used in Greek, the language of the Gospels, for 'Spirit', 'breath' and 'wind'; similarly in the language normally spoken by John and Jesus one and the same word did duty for all three concepts. The picture John draws is of the grain and the chaff lying piled up on the threshing floor after the harvest. The mixture of grain and chaff is tossed up into the air with the winnowing fork or shovel; the light chaff is blown away by the wind and the heavier grain falls back on the floor, from which it is collected to be stored in the granary. The chaff is then swept up and burned. Both the wind and the fire are symbols of the Holy Spirit; they depict the work that the Coming One is to do by the power of the Spirit, separating the true children of the kingdom from those who were only nominally so. (The figure of chaff is an ancient one in this kind of context: according to Psalm 1:4, 'The wicked ... are like chaff which the wind drives away'.)

Jesus's ministry was not exactly the ministry of judgment which John envisaged, but a ministry of sifting and separating it certainly was. Yet Jesus plainly looked for something further when he said, 'I came to set the earth on fire, and how I wish the fire had already broken out!'

One suggestion links these words with the hard saying which comes shortly afterwards in Luke 12:51–53, where Jesus says that he did not come to give peace on earth but rather division (see p. 150). We shall have to consider this hard saying also, but the difficulty about understanding his words about setting the earth on fire in the sense of the division and strife which he foresaw as the effect of his ministry lies in his earnest wish that the fire 'were already kindled'. He foresaw the division and strife indeed as the effect of his ministry, but he did not desire it. It is more satisfactory to take these words as the expression of a longing for an outpouring of the Spirit in power the like of which had not yet been seen.

Jesus himself experienced a personal outpouring of the Spirit at his baptism in the Jordan. A pictorial account of this outpouring in terms of fire is preserved in the second-century Christian writer Justin Martyr: 'When Jesus went down into the water a fire was kindled in the Jordan.'[1] The same figure appears in a saying ascribed to Jesus in the *Gospel of Thomas* and elsewhere: 'He who is near me is near the fire, and he who is far from me is far from the kingdom.'[2] The fire was there in Jesus's ministry, but the earth had not yet caught fire. One day it would catch fire in earnest, with the descent of the Holy Spirit at Pentecost; but Jesus himself had to die before this consummation could be realised, and while his death is not explicitly mentioned in these words about the fire, it is probably implied as a prospect beneath their surface. Hence the note of poignancy which can be discerned.

31.

HOW I AM CONSTRAINED UNTIL IT IS ACCOMPLISHED!

'I have a baptism to be baptised with; and how I am constrained until it is accomplished!' (Luke 12:50)

There is nothing in the immediate context of this saying, which is found only in Luke's Gospel, to throw light on its meaning. It must be read in the wider context of Jesus's whole teaching and ministry. In form it resembles the saying which precedes it, in which Jesus longs that the fire which he came to start were already kindled, but in sense it has much in common with those sayings in which the kingdom of God is seen to be subject to temporary limitations until something happens to unleash its full power. Here it is Jesus himself who is subject to a temporary limitation. As the NEB renders the saying: 'I have a baptism to undergo, and what constraint I am under until the ordeal is over!'

Two questions are raised by the saying:

1. What was the baptism which Jesus had to undergo? and

2. What was the constraint under which he had to work until this baptism had taken place?

1. There is little doubt that by his baptism he meant his impending death. This is confirmed by the record of another occasion on which he used similar language. On Jesus's last journey to Jerusalem, Mark tells us, he was approached by James and John, the two sons of Zebedee, who asked that they might be given the two positions of chief honour when his kingdom was established – the one at his right hand and the

other at his left. Their request betrayed an almost ludicrous misconception of the nature of the kingdom of which Jesus spoke, but he began to set them right by asking a question which at first did not seem to have much bearing on what they had said. 'Tell me this', he replied: 'Are you able to drink from my cup and be baptised with my baptism?' When they said, 'We are', he replied, 'You shall – but even so that will not guarantee you the two chief places for which you ask.' When he asked, 'Are you able to drink from my cup and be baptised with my baptism?' (Mark 10:38), he meant, simply, 'Are you able to share my suffering and death?' In fact, they did not share his suffering and death – not, at least, at the time when he was crucified. If things had turned out otherwise, if the crosses which flanked the cross of Jesus had been occupied not by the two robbers but by James and John, would they not have secured there and then the two positions of chief honour – the one at his right hand and the other at his left? In all subsequent Christian memory this high glory would have been exclusively theirs.

For our present purpose, however, we note that Jesus spoke then of his impending suffering and death as his 'baptism', and that supports the suggestion that the baptism to which he looked forward in the saying now under consideration bears the same meaning. If that is so, a further question arises: why did he speak of his suffering and death as a baptism? He had undergone one baptism at the beginning of his ministry, his baptism in the Jordan. Was there some feature of that baptism, administered by John the Baptist, which lent itself to this figurative use?

John's baptism is said to have been 'a baptism of repentance for the forgiveness of sins' (Mark 1:4). That is to say, people who were convicted of sin under John's preaching were invited to give public proof of their repentance by accepting baptism at his hands. Thus their sins would be forgiven and they would be 'a people prepared for the Lord' (Luke 1:17), ready for the moment when he would begin to execute his judgment through the agency of a person whom John denoted as the 'Coming One'. Jesus recognised John's ministry to be a work of God, and associated himself with it publicly by asking John to baptise him. True, Jesus at no time betrays any awareness of sin, any sense of repentance, any need for forgiveness. Yet he was never unwilling to associate with sinners: indeed, he was written off by some godly people as a 'friend of sinners' (and therefore, by implication, no better than the company he kept – see page 29). So his association with repentant sinners in receiving John's baptism was in keeping with his later practice.

Even so, some difficulty was felt about Jesus's undergoing a 'baptism of repentance for the forgiveness of sins'. Matthew in his account tells how John himself demurred at Jesus's request, saying, 'It would be more fitting that I should be baptised by you; why do you come to me?' Jesus's response to John's protest is excellently rendered in the NEB: 'Let it be so for the present; we do well to conform in this way with all that God requires' (Matt. 3:15). These words are recorded by Matthew only, but they express perfectly the spirit in which Jesus sought and received John's baptism. That this is so is confirmed by his experience when he came up from the river: he saw heaven split in two and the Spirit of God descending on him in the form of a dove, while a voice addressed him from heaven: 'You are my beloved Son; with you I am well pleased' (Mark 1:10–11). It was as though God said to him, 'You dedicate yourself to the doing of my will? You conform in this way with all that I require? I tell you this, then: you are my Son, my chosen one, the one in whom I delight.'

Jesus's period of testing in the wilderness, which followed immediately after his baptism, reinforced the strength of his commitment to do the will of God without deviation.

But what had this to do with the baptism to which he looked forward? He could, no doubt, have referred to his death, with the events leading up to it, as his baptism in the sense of a sea of troubles that threatened to overwhelm him. But in the light of the baptism which inaugurated his public ministry, we can see more in his language than that. His baptism in the Jordan gave visible expression to his resolution to fulfil the will of God, and it involved at least a token identification of himself with sinners. The ministry thus inaugurated manifested his constant devotion to the will of God and was marked by unaffected friendship with sinners. His death, which crowned that ministry, consummated his embracing of the will of God as the rule for his life, and it involved a real and personal identification of himself with sinners, on the part of one sinless himself. In this way he embodied the Old Testament picture of the obedient and suffering Servant of the Lord who 'bore the sin of many, and made intercession for the transgressors' (Isa. 53:12).

It is not for nothing that one of the latest New Testament documents voices the Christian confession in these words: 'This is he who came by water and blood, Jesus Christ – not with the water only, but with the water and with the blood' (1 John 5:6) – or, as we might say, not only with the baptism of water, but with the baptism of water and the baptism of death. The baptism of water, which inaugurated his ministry, was a faint anticipation of the baptism of death, which crowned his ministry.

2. What, then, was the constraint to which he was subject until he underwent this impending baptism? The answer to this part of our question is closely bound up with the meaning of another of Jesus's sayings at which we shall look (p. 153) – his saying about the kingdom of God coming with power (Mark 9:1). While Jesus was amply endowed with the Spirit of God for the messianic ministry which began at his baptism in the Jordan and continued until his death, his death and resurrection unleashed a power which was previously unparalleled. The limitation of which he was conscious during his ministry was due to the fact that, as it is put in the Fourth Gospel, 'As yet the Spirit had not been given, because Jesus was not yet glorified' (John 7:39).

We have spoken of his messianic ministry as lasting from his baptism in the Jordan to his death on the cross, but it would be more accurate to speak of that as the first phase of his ministry. His ministry did not come to an end with his death; he resumed it when he rose again, and continues it until now, no longer in visible presence on earth but by his Spirit in his followers. We should not think of the apostles as taking up the task which

Jesus left unfinished at his death; we should think of them rather as called to share in his still very personal ongoing ministry. This is the perspective of the New Testament writers. Luke, for example, opens the second volume of his history of Christian beginnings – the volume which we call the Acts of the Apostles – by referring back to the first volume as the record of 'all that Jesus began both to do and to teach until the day in which he was taken up' (Acts 1:1–2). The implication is that the new volume is going to tell of what Jesus *continued* to do and teach *from* the day in which he was taken up. To the same effect Paul, looking back on the major phase of his apostolic career, speaks of its very considerable achievements as 'what Christ has wrought through me to win obedience from the Gentiles, by word and deed, by the power of signs and wonders, by the power of the Holy Spirit' (Rom. 15:18–19).

The scale of the Christian achievement within a few years from the death and resurrection of Christ was out of all proportion to that of his personal achievement during his Palestinian ministry. The limitation was removed by the outpouring of the Spirit as the sequel to Christ's saving work. But without the Palestinian ministry, crowned by his death and resurrection, there would have been no such sequel, and the achievement which followed the outpouring of the Spirit was still Christ's personal achievement. He had undergone his baptism of death, and now worked on free of all restraint.

32

NOT PEACE BUT A SWORD

'Do not think that I have come to bring peace on earth;
I have not come to bring peace, but a sword' (Matt.
10:34)

This is a hard saying for all who recall the message of the angels on the night of Jesus's birth: 'Glory to God in high heaven, and peace on earth among human beings, the objects of God's favour' (as the message seems to mean). True, the angels' message appears only in Luke (2:14) and the hard saying, in the form in which we have quoted it, comes from Matthew. But Luke records the same hard saying, except that he replaces the metaphorical 'sword' by the non-metaphorical 'division' (Luke 12:51). Both evangelists then go on to report Jesus as saying, 'For I have come to set a man against his father, and a daughter against her mother, and a daughter-in-law against her mother-in-law' (Matt. 10:35; Luke 12:53), while Matthew rounds the saying off with a quotation from the Old Testament: 'a man's foes will be those of his own household' (Mic. 7:6).

One thing is certain: Jesus did not advocate conflict. He taught his followers to offer no resistance or retaliation when they were attacked or ill-treated. 'Blessed are the peace-makers,' he said, 'for they shall be called sons of God' (Matt. 5:9), meaning that God is the God of peace, so that those who seek peace and pursue it reflect his character. When he paid his last visit to Jerusalem, the message which he brought it concerned 'the things that make for peace', and he wept because the city refused his message and was bent on a course which was bound to lead to destruction (Luke 19:41-44). The message which his followers proclaimed in his name after his departure was called the 'gospel of peace' (Eph. 6:15) or the 'word of reconciliation' (2 Cor. 5:19). It was called this not merely as a matter of doctrine but as a fact of experience. Individuals and groups formerly estranged from one another found themselves reconciled through their common devotion to Christ. Something of this sort must have been experienced even earlier, in the course of the Galilean ministry: if Simon the Zealot and Matthew the tax-collector were able to live together as two of the twelve apostles, the rest of the company must have looked on this as a miracle of grace.

But when Jesus spoke of tension and conflict within a family, he probably spoke from personal experience. There are indications in the gospel story that some members of his own family had no sympathy with his ministry: the people who on one occasion tried to restrain him by force because people were saying 'He is beside himself' are called 'his friends' in the RSV but more accurately 'his family' in the NEB (Mark 3:21). 'Even his brothers did not believe in him', we are told in John 7:5. (If it is asked why, in that case, they attained positions of leadership alongside the apostles in the early Church, the answer is no doubt to be found in the statement of 1 Cor. 15:7 that Jesus, risen from the dead, appeared to his brother James.)

So, when Jesus said that he had come to bring 'not peace but a sword', he meant that this would be the *effect* of his coming, not that it was the *purpose* of his coming. His words came true in the life of the early Church, and they have verified themselves subsequently in the history of Christian missions. Where one or two members of a family or other social group have accepted the Christian faith, this has repeatedly provoked opposition from other members. Paul, who seems to have experienced such opposition in his own family circle as a result of his conversion, makes provision for similar situations in the family life of his converts. He knew that tension could arise when a husband or a wife became a Christian and the other spouse remained a pagan. If the pagan spouse was happy to go on living with the Christian, that was fine; the whole family might become Christian before long. But if the pagan partner insisted on walking out and terminating the marriage, the Christian should not use force or legal action, because 'God has called us to peace' (1 Cor. 7:12-16) – see page 61.

In these words, then, Jesus was warning his followers that their allegiance to him might cause conflict at home, and even expulsion from the family circle. It was well that they should be forewarned, for then they could not say, 'We never expected that we should have to pay *this* price for following him!'

33.

THE FALL OF SATAN

'I saw Satan fall like lightning from heaven' (Luke 10:18)

When we think of the fall of Satan, we tend to be more influenced by John Milton than by the Bible. In *Paradise Lost* Milton describes Satan and his angels being ejected from heaven and falling down to hell back in the primeval past, before the creation of the human race.

> Him the Almighty Power
> Hurl'd headlong flaming from th' Ethereal Skie
> With hideous ruin and combustion down
> To bottomless perdition, there to dwell
> In Adamantine Chains and penal Fire,
> Who durst defie th' Omnipotent to Arms.

It would be difficult to find biblical authority for this picture, however. The reader of the AV may think of Isaiah 14:12, 'How art thou fallen from heaven, O Lucifer, son of the morning!' And in truth the poetic imagery in which Lucifer's fall is depicted has been borrowed by the traditional concept of the fall of Satan. But Lucifer, son of the morning, is 'Day Star, son of Dawn' (RSV). The prophet is proclaiming the downfall of the king of Babylon, who occupied such a high place in the firmament of imperial power that his overthrow can be compared to the morning star being toppled from heaven. In the Old Testament Satan, or rather 'the satan' (the adversary), is chief prosecutor in the heavenly court, and when he fills this role he does so in the presence of God and his angels (Job 1:6–2:7; Zech. 3:1–5). See p. 147.

So when Jesus speaks of seeing Satan's fall from heaven he is not thinking of an event in the remote past. He is thinking of the effect of his ministry at the time. He had sent out seventy of his disciples to spread the announcement that the kingdom of God had drawn near, and now they had come back from their mission in great excitement. 'Why,' they said, 'even the demons are subject to us in your name!' To this Jesus replied, 'I watched how Satan fell, like lightning, out of the sky' (NEB). It is implied that he was watching for this when suddenly, like a flash of lightning, it happened; Satan plummeted – whether to earth or down to the abyss is not said.

Jesus may be describing an actual vision which he experienced during the mission of the seventy – not unlike the vision seen by John of Patmos, when, as he says, war broke out in heaven 'and the great dragon was thrown down, that ancient serpent, who is called the Devil and Satan, the deceiver of the whole world' (Rev. 12:9). When Jesus's messengers found that the demons – malignant forces that held men and women in bondage – were compelled to obey them as they commanded them, in Jesus's name, to come out of those people in whose lives they had taken up residence, this was a sign that the kingdom of God was conquering the kingdom of evil. Many of the rabbis held that, at the end of the age, God or the Messiah would overthrow Satan: the report of the seventy showed that Satan's overthrow had already taken place; and Jesus's vision of his fall from heaven confirmed this. John's Patmos version of Satan being ejected similarly indicates that his downfall was the direct result of Jesus's ministry. So too, when Jesus says in John 12:31 'Now shall the ruler of this world be cast out', the adverb 'now' refers to his impending passion, which crowned his ministry.

The downfall of Satan may be regarded as the decisive victory in the campaign; the campaign itself goes on. Hence Jesus's further words to the exultant disciples: 'I have given you authority to tread upon serpents and scorpions, and over all the power of the enemy; and nothing shall hurt you' (Luke 10:19). The 'serpents and scorpions' represent the forces of evil: thanks to the work of Christ, his people can trample them underfoot and gain the victory over them. The imagery may be borrowed from Psalm 91:13, where those who trust in God are promised that they 'will tread on the lion and the adder'. Paul uses a similar expression when he tells the Christians in Rome that, if they are 'wise as to what is good and guileless as to what is evil,' then the God of peace will soon crush Satan under their feet (Rom. 16:19–20). The wording here harks back not so much to Psalm 91 as to the story of man's first disobedience, where the serpent of Eden is told that its offspring will have its head crushed by the offspring of the woman (Gen. 3:15).

Finally, the seventy are directed not to exult in their spiritual achievements (that way lie pride and catastrophe) but to exult rather in what God has done for them.

> Rejoice not ye that sprites of ill
> Yield to your prowess in the fight;
> But joy because your Father God
> Hath writ your names elect for life.

To have one's name 'written in heaven' is to have received God's gift of eternal life.

34.

THE FATHER AND THE SON

> *'All things have been delivered to me by my Father; and
> no one knows the Son except the Father, and no one
> knows the Father except the Son, and any one to whom
> the Son chooses to reveal him'* (Matt. 11:27; cf. Luke
> 10:22)

No one would have been surprised had this saying appeared
somewhere in the Gospel of John. The language is character-
istically Johannine; the saying has been called 'an aerolite from
the Johannine heaven' or 'a boulder from the Johannine
moraine'. For all its Johannine appearance, it does not come in
the Gospel of John but in the non-Markan material common
to the Gospels of Matthew and Luke, drawn (it is widely
supposed) from the Q collection of sayings of Jesus, which may
have been in circulation not long after A.D. 50. The nearest
thing to it in the synoptic Gospels is the utterance of the risen
Christ at the end of Matthew's Gospel: 'All authority in heaven
and on earth has been given to me' (Matt. 28:18).

In both Matthew and Luke (and therefore presumably also
in the source on which they drew), the saying follows on
immediately from words in which Jesus thanks God that things
hidden from the wise and understanding have been revealed to
'babes' – that is, apparently, to the disciples. The one who has
revealed those things is Jesus himself; indeed, he is not only the
revealer of truth; he is the Son who reveals the Father. In this
context the 'all things' which have been delivered to him by the
Father would naturally be understood of the content of his

teaching or revelation. But the content of this teaching or revelation is not an abstract body of divinity; it is personal, it is God the Father himself. Jesus claims a unique personal knowledge of God, and this personal knowledge he undertakes to impart to others. Unless it is imparted by him, it is inaccessible. He is the one who at his baptism heard the Father acclaim him as his Son, his beloved, his chosen one (Mark 1:11). He enjoys a special relation and fellowship with the Father, but that relation and fellowship is open to those who learn from him. As he calls God 'Abba, Father', they may know him and call him by the same name. All the other gifts which the Father has to bestow on his children come with this personal knowledge, which is mediated by Jesus.

Matthew and Luke give the saying two different literary contexts; if we look for a historical context, we might think of some occasion when the disciples showed that they had grasped the heart of his teaching to which the minds of others remained closed, as at Caesarea Philippi.

There is nothing hard in this except to those who cannot accept the claim to uniqueness, the 'scandal of particularity', implicit in the gospel. But to those who accept the presuppositions current in a plural society this can be hard enough.

But what of the statement that 'no one knows the Son except the Father'? One line of traditional interpretation takes this to mean that the union of the divine and human natures in the one person of the Son of God is a mystery known only to the Father. But it is anachronistic to impart later christological teaching into the context of Jesus's ministry. More probably the two clauses 'no one knows the Son except the Father' and 'no one knows the Father except the Son' constitute a fuller way of saying 'no one except the Father and the Son know each other'. It has been suggested, indeed, that there is an argument from the general to the particular here – that a saying to the effect that 'only a father and a son know each other' (and therefore only the son can reveal the father) is applied to the special relation of Jesus and God: 'only the Father and the Son know each other' (and therefore only the Son can reveal the

Father). Whatever substance there may be in this suggestion, it is clear that a reciprocity of personal knowledge between the Son of God and his Father is affirmed. As none but the Father knows the Son, so none but the Son knows the Father, but the Son shares this knowledge with those whom he chooses, and in the present context that means his disciples.

There is a fascinating collection of variant readings in the textual transmission of this saying; they bear witness to difficulties which early scribes and editors found in it. The only variation at which we need to look is that between Matthew's wording and Luke's: whereas Matthew says 'knows the Son ... knows the Father', Luke says 'knows who the Son is ... or who the Father is'. Luke's wording might appear to weaken the emphasis on direct personal knowledge expressed by Matthew's wording, but this was probably not Luke's intention. If consideration be given to the Semitic construction behind the Greek of the two Gospels, Matthew's wording can claim to be closer to what Jesus actually said.

35.

YOU ARE PETER

'And I tell you, you are Peter, and on this rock I will build my church, and the powers of death shall not prevail against it. I will give you the keys of the kingdom of heaven, and whatever you bind on earth shall be bound in heaven, and whatever you loose on earth shall be loosed in heaven' (Matt. 16:18–19)

Why should this be reckoned a hard saying? It does, to be sure, contain some figures of speech which require to be explained – 'the gates of Hades' (which RSV has interpreted for us as 'the powers of death'), 'the keys of the kingdom', 'binding' and 'loosing'. But it is not because of these figures of speech that the saying is widely reckoned to be hard – so hard, indeed, that some interpreters have tried not only to explain it but to explain it away.

One reason for regarding it as a hard saying is that Peter in the Gospels is too unstable a character to serve as the foundation for any enterprise or to be given such authority as is conveyed in these words. But the main reason for finding a difficulty in the text is strictly irrelevant to its straightforward reading and interpretation. Few Protestants, asked to name their favourite text, would think of quoting this one. It has been invoked to support the supremacy of the Roman Church over other Churches – more precisely, to support the supremacy of the bishop of Rome over other bishops – and those who do not acknowledge this use of it as valid have sometimes reacted by trying to make it mean something much less positive than it appears to mean. Some have suggested, with no manuscript evidence to justify the suggestion, that the text has been corrupted from an original 'you have said' (instead of 'you are Peter'); others have argued that the Greek wording is not an accurate translation of the Aramaic form in which the saying was cast by Jesus – that what he said was, 'I tell you, Peter, that on this rock I will build my Church.' But this too is conjecture. If we can get rid of the idea that the text has any reference to the Roman Church or to the Papacy, we shall lose interest in such attempts to remove what has been felt to be its awkwardness.

Certainly there is nothing in the context to suggest Rome or the Papacy. But the context of the saying presents us with a problem of a different kind. All three synoptic evangelists record the incident in the neighbourhood of Caesarea. All of them tell how Jesus, after asking his disciples what account people were giving of him, asked them next what account they themselves gave: 'Who do you say that I am?' To this question Peter, acting as their spokesman, replied 'You are the Messiah' (that is the form of his answer in Mark 8:29; the other Gospels have variations in wording). All three evangelists add that Jesus strictly forbade them to repeat this to anyone. But Matthew inserts, between Peter's answer and Jesus's charge to the disciples not to repeat it, a personal response by Jesus to Peter. This response begins, 'Blessed are you, Simon Bar-Jona! For flesh and blood has not revealed this to you, but my Father who is in heaven.' It then continues with the words we have quoted as our hard saying.

How are we to account for the fact that the saying, with its introductory benediction, does not appear in Mark's or Luke's record of the occasion? If Matthew were the source on which Mark and Luke depended, then we could say that they abridged his record for purposes of their own, and we should try to determine what those purposes were. If, however, we are right in thinking that Mark was one of the sources on which Matthew drew, then we have to say that Matthew has amplified Mark's record by incorporating material derived from elsewhere. This is not the only place where Matthew expands Mark's record by the inclusion of material about Peter not found in our other Gospels. We may think, for example, of the episode of Peter's getting out of the boat and beginning to sink when he tried to walk to Jesus on the water (Matt. 14:28-31).

It has been argued that the passage we are considering belongs to a later period in Christian history rather than that to which Matthew assigns it. Some have seen in it the report of words spoken by Jesus to Peter when he appeared to him in resurrection – words which Matthew transferred to the Caesarea Philippi context because of the aptness of the subject-matter. Others would date them later still: is it likely, they ask, that the historical Jesus would speak of his 'church'? Certainly it is not likely that he used the word in the sense which it usually bears for us, but it is not unlikely that he used an Aramaic word which was represented in Greek by *ekklesia*, the term regularly rendered 'church' in the New Testament. And if he did, what did he mean by it? He meant the new community which he aimed to bring into being, the new Israel in which the twelve apostles were to be the leaders, leading by service and not by dictation.

A helpful analogy to Jesus's words to Peter is provided by an allegory found in rabbinical tradition setting forth God's dealings with humanity from the beginning to the time of Abraham. The written documents in which this allegory is found are later than our Gospels, but behind the written form lies a period of oral transmission. In Isaiah 51:1 Abraham is called 'the rock from which you were hewn', and the allegory undertakes to explain why Abraham should be called a 'rock'. It tells how a certain king wished to build a palace, and set his servants to dig to find a foundation. They dug for a long time, and took soundings twice, but found nothing but morass. (The soundings were taken first in the generation of Enosh, Adam's grandson, and then in the generation of Noah.) After further digging they took soundings again, and this time they struck rock (*petra*). 'Now', said the king, 'at last I can begin to build.'[1]

In the allegory the king, of course, is God; the palace which he planned to build is the nation of Israel, and he knew that he could make a beginning with the project when he found Abraham, a man ready to respond to his call with implicit faith and obedience. It would be precarious to envisage any direct relation between this allegory and Jesus's words to Peter, as recorded by Matthew, but there is a notable resemblance.

According to John's account of the call of the first disciples, it was during John the Baptist's ministry in Transjordan that Peter heard his brother Andrew say, with reference to Jesus, 'We have found the Messiah' (John 1:41). Evidently Peter then believed Andrew's testimony, but that would have been an instance of what Jesus now described as 'flesh and blood' (a human being) telling him. There were various ideas abroad in the popular mind at that time regarding the kind of person the Messiah was and the kind of things he would do, but Jesus's character and activity, as his disciples had come to know them, probably corresponded to none of those ideas. If Peter believed Jesus to be the Messiah when he first received his call, and now confessed him to be the Messiah a year or more later, the concept 'Messiah' must have begun to change its meaning for him. Not long before, he had seen his Master repel the attempt of a band of eager militants, five thousand strong, to make him their king so that he might lead them against the occupying forces of Rome and their creature, Herod Antipas (John 6:15). The Messiah as popularly conceived ought surely to have grasped such an opportunity. Some at least of the disciples were disappointed that he refused to do so.

The fact that Peter, even so, was prepared to confess Jesus as the Messiah was evidence that a change had at least begun to take place in his thinking – that he was now coming to understand the term 'Messiah' in the light of what Jesus actually was and did, rather than to understand Jesus in the light of ideas traditionally associated with the term 'Messiah'. Hence the pleasure with which Jesus greeted his response: hence the blessing which he pronounced on him. For, like the king in the Jewish parable, Jesus said in effect, 'Now at last I can begin to build!'

It is well known that 'You are Peter, and on this rock I will build my church' involves a play on words. In Greek 'Peter' is *petros* and 'rock' is *petra* (the difference being simply that between the masculine termination *-os*, necessary in a man's name, and the feminine termination *-a*). In the Aramaic which Jesus probably spoke, there was not even such a minor grammatical distinction between the two forms: 'You are *kēphā*,' he said, 'and on this *kēphā* I will build my church.' The form *kēphā*, as applied to Peter, appears in many of our New Testament versions as Cephas (e.g. in John 1:42; 1 Cor. 1:12), an alternative form of his name. As a common noun, the Aramaic *kēphā* means 'rock'; the Hebrew equivalent *kēph* is used in this sense in Job 30:6 and Jeremiah 4:29. In some modern languages the play on words can be exactly reproduced: thus in most editions of the French New Testament Jesus says to Peter, 'Tu es *Pierre*, et sur cette *pierre* je bâtirai mon église.' But this cannot be done in English; if the play on words is to be brought out, a rendering like that of the NEB has to be adopted: 'You are Peter, the Rock; and on this rock I will build my church.' Now that someone has been found who is prepared to confess Jesus as what he really is, and not try to fit him into some inherited framework, a start can be made with forming the community of true disciples who will carry on Jesus's mission after his departure.

Peter personally might be thought too unstable to provide such a foundation, but it is not Peter for what he is in himself but Peter the confessor of Jesus who provides it. In that building every other confessor of Jesus finds a place. What matters is not the stature of the confessor but the truth of the confession. Where Jesus is confessed as the Messiah or (as Matthew amplifies the wording) as 'the Christ, the Son of the living God', there his Church exists. It is in the one who is thus confessed, and not in any durable quality of her own, that the Church's security and survival rest. While she maintains that confession, the gates of the prison-house of Hades (i.e. death) will never close on her.

And what about the 'keys of the kingdom'? The keys of a royal or noble establishment were entrusted to the chief steward or major domo; he carried them on his shoulder in earlier times, and there they served as a badge of the authority entrusted to him. About 700 B.C. an oracle from God announced that this authority in the royal palace in Jerusalem was to be conferred on a man called Eliakim: 'I will place on his shoulder the key of the house of David; he shall open, and none shall shut; and he shall shut, and none shall open' (Isa. 22:22). So in the new community which Jesus was about to build, Peter would be, so to speak, chief steward. In the early chapters of Acts Peter is seen exercising this responsibility in the primitive church. He acts as chairman of the group of disciples in Jerusalem even before the coming of the Spirit at the first Christian Pentecost (Acts 1:15-26); on the day of Pentecost it is he who preaches the gospel so effectively that three thousand hearers believe the message and are incorporated in the church (Acts 2:14-41); some time later it is he who first preaches the gospel to a Gentile audience and thus 'opens a door of faith' to Gentiles as well as Jews (Acts 10:34-48). Both in Jerusalem at Pentecost and in the house of Cornelius at Caesarea, what Peter does on earth is ratified in heaven by the bestowal of the Holy Spirit on his converts. This divine confirmation was specially important in his approach to Gentiles. As Peter put it himself, 'God who knows the heart bore witness to them, giving them the Holy Spirit just as he did to us; and he made no distinction between us and them, but cleansed their hearts by faith' (Acts 15:8-9).

'Binding' and 'loosing' were idiomatic expressions in rabbinical Judaism to denote the promulgation of rulings either forbidding or authorising various kinds of activity. The authority to bind or loose given to Peter in our present context is given to the disciples as a body in Matthew 18:18, in a saying of Jesus similarly preserved by this evangelist only. Again, the record of Acts provides an illustration. Where church discipline is in view, Peter's verbal rebuke of Ananias and Sapphira received drastic ratification from heaven (Acts 5:1-11) - see p. 93. And Paul for his part, though he was not one of the disciples present when Jesus pronounced these words of authorisation, expects that when judgment is pronounced by the church of Corinth on a man who has brought the Christian name into public disrepute, at a meeting 'when you are assembled, and my spirit is present, with the power of our Lord Jesus,' the judgment will be given practical effect by God (1 Cor. 5:3–5). Again, when 'the apostles and the elders' came together in Jerusalem to consider the conditions on which Gentile believers might be recognised as fellow-members of the Church, their decision was issued as something which 'has seemed good to the Holy Spirit and to us' (Acts 15:28). Here, then, Luke may be held to provide a commentary on Matthew's record by showing how, in pursuance of Jesus's words, the keys of the kingdom were used and the power of binding and loosing was exercised in the primitive Church in preaching, discipline and legislation.

This may be added. The words in which Peter is singled out for special commendation and authority were probably handed down in a community where Peter's name was specially esteemed. The church of Antioch in Syria was one such community. There are other reasons for envisaging a fairly close association between the church of Antioch and the Gospel of Matthew, and it may well have been from material about Peter preserved at Antioch that Matthew derived these words which he incorporates into his account of what Jesus said at Caesarea Philippi.

36.

GET BEHIND ME, SATAN!

*But turning and seeing his disciples, he rebuked Peter,
and said, 'Get behind me, Satan! For you are not on the
side of God, but of men'* (Mark 8:33)

Why did Jesus address Peter with such severity?

When, in the neighbourhood of Caesarea Philippi, Peter
confessed Jesus to be the Messiah, Jesus laid a strict charge on
him and his fellow-disciples not to mention it to a soul. Why?
Probably because the title 'Messiah' (the anointed king) was
bound up in the minds of most people, and to some extent even
yet in the disciples' minds, with ideas of political rule and
military conquest, which were very far from his own
understanding of his mission in the world. If the people of
Galilee learned that Jesus's disciples considered him to be
the Messiah, their own convictions about him, which he had
done his best to dispel at the time of the feeding of the
multitude (see p. 142), would be reinforced, and this might
have disastrous results.

As for the disciples, they had to learn that, far from victory
over the Romans and a royal throne awaiting him, he faced
suffering and violent death. If they believed that he was the
Messiah, they must know what kind of Messiah he was; if they
were still minded to follow him, they must realise clearly what
kind of leader they were following, and what lay at the end of
the road he was pursuing. The revelation shocked them; this
was not what they expected. Their common sense of shock was
voiced (as usual) by Peter, who in his concern took Jesus by the

arm in a friendly gesture and began to expostulate with him: 'Mercy on you, Master! Don't speak like that. This is never going to happen to *you*!' It was to this expostulation that Jesus made his severe reply.

The words of his reply recall those with which he repelled the tempter in the wilderness, and indeed they have much the same sense here as they had there. It should be understood that 'Satan' is not primarily a proper name. It is a Hebrew common noun meaning 'adversary'. When it appears in the Old Testament preceded by the definite article, it means 'the adversary'. In the story of Job, for example, where Satan (better, 'the satan') is said to have presented himself at a session of the heavenly court (Job 1:6), the expression means 'the adversary' or, as we might say, 'counsel for the prosecution'. This is the regular function of this unpleasant character in the Old Testament. Every court must have a prosecutor, but this prosecutor enjoys his work so much that, when there are not sufficient candidates for prosecution, he goes out of his way to tempt people to go wrong, so that he may have the pleasure of prosecuting them (cf. 1 Chron. 21:1). His role as tempter is thus secondary to his role as prosecutor. The Greek word corresponding to Satan is *diabolos*, meaning 'accuser' (it is the word from which our 'devil' is derived). In Revelation 12:10, where the devil is thrown down from heaven (not at the beginning of time, as in Milton's *Paradise Lost*, but in consequence of the redemptive work of Christ – see p. 134), the holy ones in heaven rejoice because, they say, 'the accuser of our brethren has been thrown down, who accuses them day and night before our God.'

In his character as tempter he encountered Jesus in the wilderness. Jesus had just been baptised by John the Baptist and had received the assurance from God that he was his Son, his beloved one in whom he found pleasure. The language addressed to him by the voice of God (Mark 1:11) bears a fairly close resemblance to the words of Isaiah 42:1 in which God introduces the one whom he calls his servant: 'Behold my servant, whom I uphold; my chosen, in whom my soul delights.' If Jesus learned from the heavenly voice that he was to fulfil his life-mission in terms of the portrayal of the Servant of the Lord in Isaiah 42:1–4 and other passages of the same book (especially Isaiah 52:13–53:12, which similarly begins with 'Behold my servant'), then it was clear to him that the common expectation of a conquering Messiah was not going to be realised through him. Humility, obedience, suffering and death marked the way of the Father's will for him. The temptations to which he was exposed in the wilderness were calculated by the adversary to weaken his trustful obedience to God, and included the temptation to fulfil his destiny along the line of common expectation and not in accordance with what he knew to be his Father's will. We recall in particular the temptation to accept world dominion on the adversary's terms. 'It will all be yours', said he to Jesus, 'if you will fall down and worship me.' Many an ambitious man before then had yielded to that temptation, and many have yielded to it since. But Jesus repudiated the adversary's offer, and it was in his repudiation of this temptation, according to Matthew 4:10, that he said, 'Begone, Satan!' or, as many manuscripts have it, 'Get behind me, Satan!'

And now, from the lips of Peter, Jesus heard what he recognised to be the same temptation again. Peter, in effect, was trying to dissuade him from obeying his Father's will. Peter had no idea that this was what he was doing; he was moved only by affectionate concern for his Master's well-being and did not like to hear him utter such ominous words: 'The Son of man must suffer many things and be rejected' (Mark 8:31). But he was, for the moment, playing the part of an adversary, however inadvertently, for as Jesus told him, 'you are not on the side of God, but of men' (Mark 8:33).

In reproducing these words, Matthew inserts a clause not found in Mark: 'Get behind me, Satan! *You are a stumbling-block to me*, for you are not on the side of God, but of men' (Matt. 16:23). It is noteworthy that Matthew adds this reference to Peter's being a stumbling-block, since it is he alone who, in the preceding paragraph, reports Jesus's words about the rock. There are two kinds of rock here: there is a kind of rock which provides a stable foundation, and there is the kind of rock which lies in the way and trips people up. Indeed, one and the same rock can sometimes fulfil both functions. There is an oracle in Isaiah 8:13-15 where God himself is a rock which offers safe sanctuary to those who seek refuge on it in time of flood, but which will become 'a stone of offence and a rock of stumbling' to those who are swept against it by the swirling waters. Peter had it in him to be either a foundation-stone or a stumbling-block. Thanks to the intercession which his Master made for him in a critical hour, he strengthened his brethren (Luke 22:32) and became a rock of stability and a focus of unity.

37

TAKING UP THE CROSS

*'If any one would come after me, let him deny himself
and take up his cross and follow me'* (Mark 8:34)

As commonly applied, this is not a very hard saying. As
originally intended, it is very hard indeed; no saying could be
harder.

As commonly applied, the expression is used of some bodily
disability, some unwelcome experience, some uncongenial
companion or relative that one is stuck with: 'This is the cross I
have to bear', people say. It can be used in this watered-down
way because its literal sense is remote from our experience. In a
country where capital punishment is a thing of the past it is
difficult even to paraphrase it in terms of ordinary experience.

There was a time when capital punishment was not only
carried out in Britain, but carried out publicly. The condemned
criminal was led through the streets on foot or dragged on a
cart to the place of execution, and the crowds who watched this
grim procession knew what lay at the end of the road. A person
on the way to public execution was compelled to abandon all
earthly hopes and ambitions. At that time these words of Jesus
might have been rendered thus: 'If anyone wishes to come after
me, let him be prepared to be led out to public execution,
following my example.'

In all three synoptic Gospels these words follow the account
of Peter's confession at Caesarea Philippi, Jesus's first warning
about his impending passion, Peter's expostulation and the
rebuke which it drew forth from Jesus. It is as though Jesus

said to them, 'You still confess me to be the Messiah? You still wish to follow me? If so, you should realise quite clearly where I am going, and understand that, by following me, you will be going there too.' The Son of man must suffer; were they prepared to suffer with him? The Son of man faced the prospect of violent death; were they prepared to face it too? What if that violent death proved to be death on a cross? Were they prepared for that?

The sight of a man being taken to the place of public crucifixion was not unfamiliar in the Roman world of that day. Such a man was commonly made to carry the crossbeam, the *patibulum*, of his cross as he went to his death. That is the picture which Jesus's words would conjure up in the minds of his hearers. If they were not prepared for that outcome to their discipleship, let them change their minds while there was time – but let them first weigh the options in the balances of the kingdom of God: 'for whoever would save his life will lose it; and whoever loses his life for my sake and the gospel's will save it' (Mark 8:35).

Many, perhaps most, of those who heard these words proved their truth. Not all of them were actually crucified. This, we know, was Peter's lot; the first of those present to suffer death for Jesus's sake, James the son of Zebedee, was beheaded (Acts 12:2). But this is what is meant by 'taking up the cross' – facing persecution and death for Jesus's sake.

When Luke reproduces this saying he amplifies it slightly: 'let him deny himself and take up his cross *daily*' (Luke 9:23). A later disciple of Jesus, one who was not present to hear these words in person, entered fully into their meaning and emphasises this aspect: 'I die every day', Paul writes (1 Cor. 15:31), meaning 'I am exposed to the risk of death every day, and that for Jesus's sake.' He speaks of himself and his fellow-apostles as 'always carrying in the body the dying of Jesus' and explains himself by saying that 'while we live we are always being given up to death for Jesus' sake, so that the life of Jesus may be manifested in our mortal flesh' (2 Cor. 4:10–11). In another place he refers to 'the surpassing worth of knowing Christ Jesus my Lord' for whose sake he has suffered the loss of everything, and tells how his consuming ambition is 'that I may know him and the power of his resurrection, and may share his sufferings, becoming like him in his death' (Phil. 3:8, 10). As a Roman citizen, Paul was not liable to be crucified, but he knew by experience what it meant to 'take up his cross daily' and follow Jesus.

Jesus's words about the necessity of denying oneself if one wishes to be his disciple are to be understood in the same sense. Here too is a phrase that has become unconscionably weakened in pious phraseology. Denying oneself is not a matter of giving up something, whether for Lent or for the whole of life: it is a decisive saying 'No' to oneself, to one's hopes and plans and ambitions, to one's likes and dislikes, to one's nearest and dearest (see p. 121), for the sake of Christ. It was so for the first disciples, and it is so for many disciples today. But if this is how it is to be taken – and this is how it was meant to be taken – it is a hard saying indeed.

Yet to some disciples it might be encouraging at the same time – to those actually being compelled to suffer for their Christian faith. The Gospel of Mark was probably written in the first instance for Christians in Rome who were enduring unforeseen and savage persecution under the Emperor Nero in the aftermath of the great fire of A.D. 64. For some of them this persecution involved literal crucifixion. It was reassuring for them to be reminded that their Lord himself had said that this kind of experience was only to be expected by his disciples. If they were suffering for his name's sake, this meant that they were sharers in his suffering; it meant also that they were truly his disciples and would be acknowledged as such by him in the presence of God.

38.

THE KINGDOM COMING WITH POWER

'Truly, I say to you, there are some standing here who will not taste death before they see that the kingdom of God has come with power' (Mark 9:1)

To say that some who are now present will not die before a certain event takes place is the same thing as saying that the event will take place within 'this generation' (see p. 225). What, then, is the event in question – the coming of the kingdom of God, 'with power'?

The kingdom of God, the new order which Jesus came to inaugurate, had drawn near when he began his public ministry in Galilee: this was the burden of his preaching at that time (Mark 1:14–15). Its presence was manifested by his works of mercy and power, especially by his healing of the demon-possessed: 'If it is by the finger of God that I cast out demons,' he said, 'then the kingdom of God has come upon you' (Luke 11:20). But evidently it had not yet come 'with power' as it would come one day in the foreseeable future. At present it was subject to limitations, but the time would come when those limitations would be removed and it would advance unchecked (see p. 128).

What, we may ask, had Jesus in mind when he made this prediction? And can we recognise its fulfilment in any event or development recorded in the New Testament? We can; but before we try to do so, let us think of a parallel set of sayings. Jesus sometimes spoke of the kingdom of God; he sometimes spoke of the Son of man. He rarely used the two expressions together, but each implies the other. It is the Son of man who introduces the kingdom of God, the Son of man being Jesus himself. There are two sets of sayings about the Son of man in the Gospels which stand in contrast to one another. In the one set the Son of man is exposed to humiliation and suffering; in the other he is vindicated and glorified. His vindication is sometimes described pictorially as his being enthroned at the right hand of God. This expression is derived from Psalm 110:1, where the divine invitation is extended to a royal personage: 'Sit at my right hand' – the right hand of God being the position of supreme honour and power. Thus, standing before his judges, on the point of receiving the death sentence from them, Jesus assures them that 'from now on the Son of man shall be seated at the right hand of the power of God' (Luke 22:69; see p. 247).

His death marked the end of his humiliation and suffering and, with his resurrection, ushered in his vindication. As a later Christian confession put it, he 'was manifested in the flesh, vindicated in the Spirit' (1 Tim. 3:16). And this transition from the Son of man's humiliation to his vindication corresponds exactly to the transition from the kingdom of God subject to temporary limitations to the kingdom of God now present 'with power'. The same phrase 'with power' (or 'in power') is used by Paul when he speaks of Jesus as 'descended from David according to the flesh' but 'designated Son of God in power according to the Spirit of holiness by his resurrection from the dead' (Rom. 1:3–4).

With the death and exaltation of Jesus and the coming of the Spirit on the day of Pentecost following, some of those who were witnesses of his mighty works in Galilee and elsewhere saw the power of the kingdom of God manifested on a scale unmatched during his ministry. Within a few weeks, the number of his followers multiplied tenfold; his kingdom was visibly on the march.

This, at any rate, is an interpretation of his saying about the kingdom of God having come with power which makes it intelligible to us. Whether or not this interpretation coincides with his intention when he spoke in this way is a question to which it is best not to give a dogmatic answer.

The three evangelists who record the saying (in varying terms) go on immediately to describe Jesus's transfiguration, as though that event bore some relation to the saying (Matt. 17:1–8; Mark 9:2–8; Luke 9:28–36). It cannot be said that the transfiguration was the event which Jesus said would come within the lifetime of some of his hearers: one does not normally use such language to refer to something that is to take place in a week's time. But the three disciples who witnessed the transfiguration had a vision of the Son of man vindicated and glorified: they saw in graphic anticipation the fulfilment of his words about the powerful advent of the kingdom of God. Matthew, strikingly, in his report of the words speaks of the Son of man instead of the kingdom of God: 'there are some standing here who will not taste death before they see the Son of man coming in his kingdom' (Matt. 16:28). This is an interpretation of the words, but a true interpretation. And Matthew follows Mark in saying that, when the disciples had seen the vision, Jesus forbade them to speak about it to anyone 'until the Son of man should have risen from the dead' (Mark 9:9). His rising from the dead would inaugurate the reality which they had seen in vision on the mount of transfiguration, and would at the same time herald the coming of the kingdom 'with power'.

One final point: the coming oı the kingdom of God is essentially the coming of God himself. In the Targum (the Aramaic rendering of the Hebrew Bible used in synagogue services) the wording at the end of Isaiah 40:9 is changed from 'Behold your God!' to 'The kingdom of your God is revealed.' The documentary evidence for this rendering is much later than the New Testament period, but it reflects rabbinical usage. When the God of Israel overruled the course of events so as to bring his people home from exile, it might be said that his sovereign power (his 'kingdom') was manifested, but what the prophet said was more direct: 'Behold your God!' In the course of events which led to Israel's return from exile, God himself was to be seen. So again, when the new deliverance was fully accomplished by the death and triumph of Jesus, the sovereign power of God was manifested – God himself came with power.

39.

FOR OR AGAINST

'He who is not with me is against me, and he who does not gather with me scatters' (Matt. 12:30; Luke 11:23)
'He that is not against us is for us' (Mark 9:40; cf. Luke 9:50)

There is no formal contradiction between 'He who is not with me is against me' and 'He that is not against us is for us' (or, as Luke has it, 'he that is not against you is for you'). In a situation where no neutrality is possible, people must be either on one side or on the other, so that those who are not for are against, and those who are not against are for. But there is a difference in emphasis between the two ways of expressing this.

The former saying comes in a context where Jesus is speaking of the conflict between the kingdom of God and the forces of evil. This is a conflict in which no one should be neutral. Since Jesus is the divinely appointed agent for leading the battle against the forces of evil, those who wish to see the triumph of God's cause must follow him. If they do not, then whatever they may think themselves, they are effectively on the enemy's side. As for the added words about gathering and scattering, gathering is the work of God, while scattering is the work of Satan. God is the God of peace; Satan is the author of strife. 'The Kingdom of God is the one constructive unifying redemptive power in a distracted world; and every man has to choose whether he will take sides with it or against it.'[1]

The latter saying is related to the same subject, although it comes in the course of a narrative, as the punch-line in what is sometimes called a 'pronouncement story'. The story is told, that is to say, for the sake of the pronouncement to which it leads up. Here, then, we have such a punch-line. John, one of the two 'sons of thunder' (as Jesus called him and his brother James because of their stormy temperament), tells Jesus that he and his companions saw someone casting out demons in Jesus's name, 'and we forbade him, because he was not following us' (Mark 9:38). In other words, he was not one of the regularly recognised disciples of Jesus. But he was showing clearly which side he was on in the spiritual warfare; moreover, he was acknowledging the authority of Jesus, because it was in his name that he was casting out demons. This was a far cry from the spirit that ascribed Jesus's demon-expelling power to the aid of Beelzebul. By his words and actions he was showing himself to be on Jesus's side.

John was no doubt concerned lest his Master's name might be taken in vain, if it was invoked by a man who had not been authorised by Jesus to speak or act in his name. But Jesus did not share his well-meant concern. John has always had his successors in the Church, who feel unhappy when things are done in Jesus's name by people whose authority to do them they cannot recognise. But Jesus's reply remains sufficient to silence this attitude: 'no one who does a mighty work in my name will be able soon after to speak evil of me' (Mark 9:39).

40

THE SON OF MAN HAS NOWHERE TO LAY HIS HEAD

'Foxes have holes, and the birds of the air have nests; but the Son of man has nowhere to lay his head' (Matt. 8:20; Luke 9:58)

This saying comes in the first of a series of interviews (two in Matthew, three in Luke) between Jesus and would-be disciples. It can be called a hard saying only in the sense that it warned the would-be disciple of the hardships that would be involved in following Jesus. For the man – a scribe, or expert interpreter of the law, according to Matthew – was not volunteering to become a follower of Jesus in the general sense of following his teaching; he proposed to join his company on a permanent footing: 'I will follow you wherever you go', he said. Jesus warned him that, while wild animals have places where they can rest by night (the foxes in their dens and the birds in their nests), he himself did not know from day to day as he moved around the country where he would find shelter, or even if he would find shelter, for the next night; and his companions must be prepared to share the same uncertain lot. This lack of any place which he could call his own was only one aspect of the humiliation of the Son of man – a humiliation which many of the disciples found it hard to accept.

The saying has been made harder than it really is by attempts to understand the phrase 'the Son of man' as something more (or less) than a way of referring to Jesus himself. One suggestion is that the phrase here simply means 'man' in general, and that its application to Jesus is secondary. That is to say, the saying is in origin a proverb meaning that wild animals have their natural resting-places but man is homeless. There is no evidence for the currency of such a proverb, and in any case it would not be true.

Another suggestion was made by T. W. Manson, in line with his view that 'the Son of man' in the teaching of Jesus primarily denoted God's elect community, the true believing Israel, which Jesus was constituting around himself (and which, in the crucial hour, was embodied in Jesus himself). If 'the Son of man' has this corporate sense in the present saying, then the foxes and the birds might be expected to have a comparable sense. He proposed therefore, tentatively, to understand the saying thus: 'everybody is at home in Israel's land except the true Israel. The birds of the air (the Roman overlords), the foxes (the Edomite interlopers), have made their position secure. The true Israel is disinherited by them: and if you cast your lot with me and mine you join the ranks of the dispossessed, and you must be prepared to serve God under those conditions.'[1] (The 'Edomite interlopers' were the Herods; Herod Antipas, the ruler of Galilee, is described by Jesus as 'that fox' in Luke 13:32.) But it is unlikely that the would-be disciple would have understood those allusions; it is best to take the words about the Son of man as referring to Jesus himself. 'The saying refers to the continuing hardship and loneliness involved in *following* the Son of Man'.[2]

41.

LET THE DEAD BURY THEIR DEAD

'Leave the dead to bury their own dead; but as for you,
go and proclaim the kingdom of God' (Luke 9:60)

These words belong to the second in the group of three incidents in which Jesus impresses on potential followers the absolute priority of the claims of the kingdom of God over everything else. Here he calls on a man to come along with him as his disciple. The man is not unwilling, but says, 'let me first go and bury my father'. A reasonable request, one might have thought: burial took place very soon after death, so, if his father had just died, he would probably be buried the same day. The man would then be free to follow Jesus. If he was the eldest son, it was his responsibility to see to his father's burial. It may be, however, that he meant, 'Let me stay at home until my father dies; when I have buried him, I shall be free of family obligations, and then I will come and follow you.' This is not the most natural way to take his words, although it makes Jesus's response less peremptory. But an interpretation which makes Jesus's demands less peremptory than they seem to be at first blush is probably to be rejected for that very reason. His demands *were* peremptory.

Who then are 'the dead' who are to be left to bury the dead? One suggestion is that Jesus's Aramaic words have been mistranslated into Greek – that he actually meant, 'Leave the dead to the burier of the dead.' That is to say, there are people whose professional work it is to bury the dead; they can be left to look after this business, but there is more important work for you to do. But this again detracts from the rigorous peremptoriness of Jesus's words. They are best taken to mean, 'Leave the (spiritually) dead to bury the (physically) dead' – there are people who are quite insensitive to the claims of the kingdom of God, and they can deal with routine matters like the burial of the dead, but those who are alive to its claims must give them the first place. T. W. Manson thought that Jesus's reply was a vivid way of saying, 'That business must look after itself; you have more important work to do.'[1]

The burial even of dead strangers was regarded as a highly meritorious work of piety in Judaism; how much more the burial of one's own kith and kin! Attendance to the duty of burying one's parents was held to be implied in the fifth commandment: 'Honour your father and mother.' It took precedence over the most solemn religious obligations. But so important in Jesus's eyes was the business of following him and promoting the kingdom of God that it took precedence even over the burial of the dead.

The added words in Luke 9:60, 'but as for you, go and proclaim the kingdom of God', are absent from the parallel in Matthew 8:22. The proclamation that the kingdom of God had drawn near was part of the charge which Jesus laid on his disciples (Luke 9:2; 10:9). The direct sense of his injunction to this man is related to the circumstances of his Galilean ministry, but it retained its relevance after his death and resurrection, and a situation may arise in which it proves still to be strikingly relevant.

John McNeill, a well-known Scottish preacher of a past generation, used to tell how he found this saying directly relevant to him. When his father died in Scotland, towards the end of the nineteenth century, he was in the English Midlands, and was advertised to address an evangelistic meeting in a certain city on the very day of his father's funeral. People would have understood had he sent a message to say that he was compelled to cancel his engagement. 'But I dared not send it,' he said, 'for this same Jesus stood by me, and seemed to say,

"Now, look, I have you. You go and preach the gospel to those people. Whether would you rather bury the dead or raise the dead?" And I went to preach.'[2]

42.

LOOKING BACK

'No one who puts his hand to the plough and looks back is fit for the kingdom of God' (Luke 9:62)

This is the third response of Jesus to a would-be disciple: Luke has brought the three together into one context. There is no parallel to this response in Matthew's record, as there is to its two predecessors.

'I will follow you, Lord,' said this man, 'but let me first say farewell to those at my home.' The words 'I will follow you, *but* ...' have served as the text for many a powerful sermon, but in the present instance the 'but' was not unreasonable and could indeed claim a venerable precedent. Over 800 years before, the prophet Elijah was divinely commanded to enlist Elisha the son of Shaphat to be his colleague and successor. As Elijah went to do so, he found Elisha ploughing with oxen. He said nothing, but threw his cloak over the young man as he passed. The young man knew immediately what the prophet's gesture meant, ran after him and said, 'Let me kiss my parents goodbye; then I will come with you.' 'Go back', said Elijah; 'what have I done to you?' But Elisha would not be put off; he knew that Elijah had called him to go with him, but did not wish to put any pressure on him; the response to his gesture must be Elisha's spontaneous choice. So Elisha went back and not only said goodbye to his father and mother, but made a sumptuous farewell feast for all who lived or worked on their family farm; he killed two oxen, cooked their flesh on a fire made with the wood of their yoke, and after he had entertained the people in this way he 'went after Elijah, and ministered to him' (1 Kgs. 19:19–21).

Elijah was a very important person, outstandingly engaged in the service of the God of Israel, but he offered no objection to Elisha's taking time to bid his family and friends farewell in a suitable manner. But the business of the kingdom of God, on which Jesus was engaged, was much more urgent than Elijah's business, and brooked no such delay. Once again it is evident that, in Jesus's reckoning, family ties must take second place to the kingdom which he proclaimed.

Jesus's reply, like the story of Elisha's call, has a reference to ploughing, but this is probably coincidental. In any agricultural society we might expect a proverbial saying about the importance of looking straight ahead when one's hand has been put to the plough: the ploughman who looks back will not drive a straight furrow. Jesus may well have adapted such a saying: the ploughman who looks back is unfit for the kingdom of God. Here the ploughman who looks back is the would-be disciple whose mind is still partly on the life he left to follow Jesus. The work of the kingdom of God requires singleness of purpose.

Sometimes a reference has been detected here to Lot's wife, whose backward look as she and her family fled from the destruction of Sodom was her undoing (Gen. 19:26). This reference is unlikely in the present context. On another occasion Jesus did say 'Remember Lot's wife' (Luke 17:32), but that was when he was warning his hearers to flee from a future destruction comparable with that which overtook Sodom.

43.

I WILL WARN YOU WHOM TO FEAR

'I tell you, my friends, do not fear those who kill the body, and after that have no more that they can do. But I will warn you whom to fear: fear him who, after he has killed, has power to cast into hell; yes, I tell you, fear him!' (Luke 12:4–5; cf. Matt. 10:28)

The first part of this saying presents no difficulty. Jesus faced violent death himself, and warned his disciples more than once that they might expect no less. 'Brother will deliver up brother to death,' he said, '. . . and you will be hated by all for my name's sake' (Matt. 10:21–22). In a counterpart to these words in the Fourth Gospel he tells them that 'the hour is coming when whoever kills you will think he is offering service to God' (John 16:2). But those who put them to death could do them no more harm. Stephen might be stoned to death, but his eyes were filled with the vision of the Son of man standing to welcome him as his advocate and friend at the right hand of God (Acts 7:55–60). So too Paul, on the eve of execution, could say with confidence, 'The Lord will rescue me from every evil and save me for his heavenly kingdom' (2 Tim. 4:6–18).

It is the second part of the saying that raises a question. Whereas in both Gospels 'those who kill the body' are referred to in the plural, the person who is really to be feared is mentioned in the singular: it is he 'who, after he has killed, has power to cast into hell' or, as it is put in Matthew's version, 'who can destroy both soul and body in hell' (Matt. 10:28). Who is he?

There are those who 'kill the body but cannot kill the soul', as it runs in Matthew; there are others who do serious damage to the souls of men, women and children by reducing them to obedient automata, by leading them into sin, or in other ways. Are such people more to be feared than ordinary murderers? Perhaps they are. The singular pronoun 'him' in 'fear him!' could mean 'that sort of person'. But it is more probable that Jesus meant, 'Be more afraid of the condemnation of God than of the death-sentence of human beings.' This sense is not unparalleled in Jewish literature of the period. In a document from Jewish Alexandria, the fourth book of Maccabees (which quite certainly has not influenced the present saying of Jesus or been influenced by it), seven brothers about to be martyred because of the refusal to renounce their faith encourage one another in these words: 'Let us not fear him who thinks he is killing us; for great conflict and danger to the soul is laid up in eternal torment for those who transgress the commandment of God' (4 Macc. 13:14–15). If they are put to death for their fidelity to God, they have the sure hope of eternal life; if through fear of physical death they prove unfaithful to him, certain retribution awaits them. The sense is more or less the same in Jesus's present saying. The one who has power to cast into hell is not, as some have suggested, the devil; if he is resisted, he can do no real harm to the follower of Jesus. It is God who is to be feared:

> Fear him, ye saints, and you will then
> Have nothing else to fear.

The 'hell' mentioned here is Gehenna, the place of eternal destruction after death. There are Jewish parallels for the belief, attested in Matthew's form of the saying, that soul and body alike are consumed in the fire of Gehenna.

It is noteworthy that in both Gospels, immediately after the warning that the condemnation of God is to be feared, comes the encouragement that the protecting love of God is to be trusted: the God who takes note of the fall of a single sparrow knows every hair of his children's heads (Luke 12:6-7; Matt. 10:29-31).

44.

THE ELDER BROTHER

'Now his elder son ... was angry and refused to go in'
(Luke 15:25–28)

The prodigal's elder brother deserves our sympathy. He had never given his father a moment's anxiety, but no fuss was ever made over him. Of course not; no one makes a fuss over people who are always at hand and always dependable. The tendency is rather to take them for granted, and those who are always being taken for granted become aware of the fact and do not like it.

How different it was with the younger son! His original request was reasonable: for the two sons to share the family smallholding would probably not have worked. It was better that he should get his share of the inheritance in cash, and seek his living elsewhere. His was in any case the smaller share; the elder son would get his double portion in land.

The trouble arose when the younger son squandered his money instead of investing it wisely. The day of reckoning was bound to come for him. For a Jew to be reduced to looking after a Gentile's pigs was degradation indeed; yet he would gladly have joined the pigs at the feeding-trough for a share in the carob-bean pods which they munched, so hungry was he. To go back and beg for employment as a casual labourer on his father's land was humiliating, but he could think of nothing better. Casual labourers might earn but a denarius a day (see p. 196), but that was probably more than he was getting from the pig-owner; and while they were there, they could eat as much as they wanted. So he swallowed his pride and went back.

The father might have said, 'That's all very well, young man; we have heard fine speeches before. Now you buckle to and get down to work as you have never worked before, and if we see that you really mean what you say, we may let you work your passage. But you can never make good the damage you have done to the family's good name and property.' That in itself would have been an act of grace; it might have done the young man a world of good, and his elder brother would probably not have objected. But – and this is the point of the parable – that is not how God treats sinners. He does not put them on probation first, to see how they will turn out. He welcomes them with overflowing love and generosity. And Jesus, in befriending such undesirable types as he did, was displaying the generous love of God (see p. 30).

Those who entered into theological controversy with Jesus would not have denied that God was like that. In a later rabbinical work God is represented as saying to the Israelites, 'Open to me a gateway of repentance only as wide as the eye of a needle, and I will drive chariots and horses through it.'[1] But it is not always easy to put theological theory into practice. They might magnify the grace of God, as we may do, but does it not seem prudent to put repentant sinners on probation first? Can they be admitted to the holy table, not to speak of our own tables at home, without more ado?

That is how the prodigal's elder brother felt. He had stayed at home all the time, led a blameless life, worked on the farm, carried out his father's direction. It had not occurred to him to expect much in the way of appreciation until the black sheep of the family turned up with his hard-luck story and the occasion was celebrated with an evening's feasting and jollification – the fatted calf killed, the neighbours invited in, music and dancing and no expense spared!

But life is like that. As the parables of the lost sheep and the lost coin showed, more fuss is made over the recovery of something that was lost than over the safe keeping of what has been there all the time, and where human beings are concerned, this is even more so.

There are young people who have come up through Sunday School and Bible Class, who join the church and are present week by week at all the meetings – perhaps notice is taken of them, perhaps not. But here is a rank outsider – a Borstal alumnus, maybe – who has been dragged along to a Billy Graham meeting or something of the sort and has gone forward when the appeal was made; and what a fuss is made of him! He is billed at every youth rally, invited to give his testimony at every opportunity (and it must be admitted that his testimony is rather more colourful than that of someone who has never strayed from the straight and narrow) – but if some people feel that it is all really sickening one can understand their point of view.

No blame is attached to the elder brother; he remains sole heir to all his father's property. He simply does not feel the way his father does about the prodigal's return. A human father feels that way, and the heavenly Father feels that way. 'There will be more joy in heaven over one sinner who repents than over ninety-nine righteous persons who need no repentance' (Luke 15:7). No blame attaches to the ninety-nine; of course not. But they were never lost; that is what makes the difference.

45.

WHY DO YOU CALL ME GOOD?

'Why do you call me good? No one is good but God alone' (Mark 10:18; Luke 18:19)

This is not a very hard saying. Schmiedel, however, included it in his list of pillar texts, arguing (quite cogently) that it is most likely to come from Jesus himself, since no one else was likely to put into his mouth words which seemed to cast doubt on his goodness. A would-be disciple (a rich man, as the sequel shows, but that is irrelevant at this point) ran up to Jesus once and said, 'Good Teacher, what must I do to inherit eternal life?' Before answering his question, Jesus took him up on his use of the epithet 'good'. A word which in its proper sense belonged to God alone should not be used lightly as a mere expression of courtesy, and Jesus suspected that it was simply as a polite form of address that the man used it. He himself did not refuse to describe people as good when he really meant 'good'. If it be asked how such language squares with his assertion here that 'No one is good but God alone', the answer is plain: no one is altogether good, as God is, but men and women are good in so far as they reflect the goodness of God.

It appears, indeed, that the form in which Mark (followed by Luke) preserves these words of Jesus was felt to present a difficulty at quite an early stage in the formation of the Gospels. In the parallel passage in Matthew 19:16–17 the weight of the textual evidence favours the recasting of the man's question as 'Teacher, what good deed must I do, to have eternal life?' – to which Jesus replies, 'Why do you ask me about what is good? One there is who is good.' This recasting of the question and answer, however, was not perpetuated. Whereas normally, in the process of transmitting the Gospel text, the tendency is for the wording of the other evangelists to be conformed to that of Matthew, here the Matthaean wording has been conformed to that of Mark and Luke in the majority of later manuscripts, followed by the AV: '"Good Master, what good thing shall I do, that I may have eternal life?" . . . "Why callest thou me good? there is none good but one, that is, God."' If the saying had been felt to be insuperably hard, the Matthaean form would have prevailed throughout the synoptic record of the incident.

46.

SELL WHAT YOU HAVE

*'You lack one thing; go, sell what you have, and give to
the poor, and you will have treasure in heaven; and
come, follow me'* (Mark 10:21)

The man to whom these words were spoken certainly found
them hard. He was the rich man who came to Jesus and asked
what he should do to inherit eternal life. Jesus said, 'Well, you
know the commandments', and mentioned those which sum up
one's duty to a neighbour. That keeping the commandments
was the way to life is stated in the law itself: 'You shall therefore
keep my statutes and my ordinances, by doing which a man
shall live: I am the Lord' (Lev. 18:5). The man answered that he
had kept all these from early days – presumably ever since the
age of thirteen, when he became *bar mitzvah*, personally
responsible to keep the commandments.

But he plainly expected Jesus to say something more: he did
not come to him just to learn that keeping the commandments
was the way to life. And the something more that he waited for
came quickly: 'There is one thing you haven't done', Jesus said,
'and you can do it now: sell your property, give the poor the
money you get for it, and come and join my disciples. You will
get rid of the burden of material goods, and you will be laying
up treasure in heaven.' But the man, an honest and attractive
character evidently, found this counsel too hard to accept. It is
sometimes called a counsel of perfection, from the way in
which another evangelist phrases it: 'If you would be perfect,
go, sell what you possess and give to the poor' (Matt. 19:21).

But this does not mean that keeping the commandments is the duty of all, whereas giving all their goods to feed the poor is the privilege of those who would attain a higher level of devotion. Paul reminds us that even giving all our goods to feed the poor is worthless without love in the heart (1 Cor. 13:3). Matthew's wording might be rendered: 'If you want to go the whole way in fulfilling the will of God, this is what you must do.'

For those who wish to treat the teaching of Jesus seriously and make it, as far as possible, their rule of life, this is still a hard saying. It is easy to say, 'This is how he tested one man's devotion, but he did not ask all his hearers to give away their property in the same way.' It is true that those who joined his company and went around with him as his disciples appear to have left all to follow him. But what of those friends by whose generosity they were maintained – those well-to-do women who, as Luke tells us, 'provided for them out of their means' (Luke 8:3)? They were not asked to make the sacrifice that our rich man was asked to make; it might be said, of course, that they were doing something of the same kind by supplying Jesus and the twelve out of their resources. When Jesus invited himself to a meal in the house of the chief tax-collector of Jericho, no pressure apparently was put on Zacchaeus to make his spontaneous announcement: 'Behold, Lord, the half of my goods I give to the poor' (Luke 19:8). It is usually inferred that this was to be his practice from that time on; it is just possible, however, that he meant that this was what he regularly did. Either way, Jesus recognised him as a 'son of Abraham' in the true sense, a man of faith. But he did not tell him to get rid of the other half of his goods as well, nor did he suggest that he should quit his tax-collecting and join his company, as another tax-collector had done in Capernaum at an earlier date.

Even so, Jesus's advice to the rich man is by no means isolated; it is a regular feature of his teaching. The same note is struck in words appearing without a narrative context in Luke 12:33–34: 'Sell your possessions, and give alms; provide yourselves with purses that do not grow old, with a treasure in the heavens that does not fail, where no thief approaches and no moth destroys. For where your treasure is, there will your heart be also.' Matthew includes the same message in his version of the Sermon on the Mount (Matt. 6:19–21), in a rhythmical form which may have been designed for easy memorising:

> Do not lay up for yourselves treasures on earth,
>> where moth and rust consume,
>> and where thieves break in and steal;
> but lay up for yourselves treasures in heaven,
>> where neither moth nor rust consumes,
>> and where thieves do not break in and steal.
>>> For where your treasure is,
>>> there will your heart be also.

(If an attempt is made to turn these words from the Greek in which the evangelist has preserved them back into the Aramaic in which they were spoken, they display not only poetical rhythm but even rhyme.)

This teaching was not given to one special individual; it was intended for Jesus's followers in general. He urged them to have the right priorities, to seek God's kingdom and righteousness above all else (Matt. 6:33). But it is very difficult to do this, he maintained, if one's attention is preoccupied by material wealth. Experience shows that some wealthy men and women have promoted the kingdom of God above their worldly concerns – that they have, indeed, used their worldly concerns for the promotion of his kingdom. But experience also shows that their number is very small. There is something about concentration on material gain which not only encroaches on the time and energy that might otherwise be devoted to the interests of the kingdom of God; it makes one less concerned about those interests, less disposed to pay attention to them. Naturally so: Jesus was stating a law of life when he said that where one's treasure is, there the heart will be also. He would clearly have liked to enrol the rich man among his disciples, and up to a point the rich man was not unwilling to become one of them. But the sticking point came when he was asked to unburden himself of his property.

Fulness to such a burden is
That go on pilgrimage.[1]

But he decided that he would sooner go on bearing his burden
than become a pilgrim. Jesus's words to him were not intended
for him alone; they remain as a challenge, a challenge not to be
evaded, for all who wish to be his disciples.

47

GIVE FOR ALMS WHAT IS WITHIN

'But give for alms those things which are within; and behold, everything is clean for you' (Luke 11:41)

This is a hard saying in the sense that it is not easily understood. Other sayings about giving alms are hard in the sense that, while their meaning is all too plain, it goes against the grain to put them into action. 'Sell your possessions, and give alms' (Luke 12:33) is one of these; not even the assurance that this is a way of laying up treasure in heaven makes it altogether easy to comply with it. But what are the 'things which are within' that are to be given for alms?

This saying comes in a context where Jesus rebukes some religious people for insisting on the external forms of religious practice while overlooking the inward and essential realities. No amount of ritual washing of the hands or other parts of the body will be of any avail if the heart is not pure. Only a foolish person would be careful to wash the outside of a cup or dish after use and pay no attention to the inside; the inside generally requires more careful washing than the outside. It is even more foolish to pay meticulous heed to external observances when inwardly one is 'full of extortion and wickedness'. What, then, is the point of the immediately following exhortation, 'But give the things inside for alms'? How will that make 'everything . . . clean for you'?

If one looks at the Greek text, the first clause of Luke 11:41 could be translated differently: 'But give for alms those things that are within your control (or at your disposal)'. Could this go well with the next clause: 'and behold, everything is clean for you'? It might: this would not be the only text in the Bible to imply that almsgiving is a means of ethical purification. Daniel, impressing on King Nebuchadnezzar the urgent necessity of mending his ways, advised him: 'break off your sins by practising righteousness [which may well mean almsgiving], and your iniquities by showing mercy to the oppressed' (Dan. 4:27).

But could the rendering 'give for alms those things that are within your control' go well with what precedes? It might be argued that, since Jesus had just mentioned extortion as one of the things which pollute a person's inner life, almsgiving, which is the opposite of extortion, would have a cleansing instead of a polluting effect. Even so, the flow of thought is not smooth.

Luke's form of the saying, however, cannot be considered in isolation from the parallel text in Matthew 23:26. There too the words come in the course of criticism of those Pharisees who, as Jesus says, 'cleanse the outside of the cup and of the plate, but inside . . . are full of extortion and rapacity'. Then comes his direction: 'first cleanse the inside of the cup and of the plate, that the outside also may be clean'. First things first, in other words. But the difficulty raised by Luke's form of the saying has disappeared: 'first cleanse the inside' is much more intelligible than 'give what is inside for alms'.

Has Matthew eased a difficult construction which Luke left unchanged, as he found it? That is possible. But another possibility is pointed out by some scholars. Whereas Matthew and Luke seem at times to use the same Greek translation of the Q sayings, there are other times when they use different translations of one Aramaic original. Here 'cleanse' and 'give alms' could be translations of two quite similar Aramaic verbs; they could even be alternative translations of one and the same Aramaic verb, in two different senses. This could be the explanation of the difference between the versions of Matthew and Luke, but since the original Aramaic wording of the saying has not survived, the explanation must remain speculative.

48

THE CAMEL AND THE EYE OF A NEEDLE

*'It is easier for a camel to go through the eye of a needle
than for a rich man to enter the kingdom of God'*
(Mark 10:25)

This saying is paralleled in Matthew 19:24 and Luke 18:25. In
all three synoptic Gospels it follows the incident of the rich man
who was anxious to know how to inherit eternal life – and, in
the idiom of the Gospels, inheriting eternal life is synonymous
with entering the kingdom of God. His record in keeping the
commandments was unimpeachable – he assured Jesus that he
had kept them all ever since he came to years of discretion, and
Jesus said nothing to suggest that his claim was exaggerated.
But, to test the strength of his commitment, Jesus bade him sell
his property and distribute the proceeds among the poor.
'Then', he said, 'you will have treasure in heaven; and come,
follow me.' At that the rich man's face fell: this sacrifice was
more than he was prepared to make. The incident brings out
the radical nature of the discipleship to which Jesus called
people.

Then, to illustrate 'how hard it is for those who have riches to
enter the kingdom of God' he used this striking figure of
speech. His hearers recognised it immediately to be a hard
saying. It is not merely difficult, it is impossible for a rich man
to get into the kingdom of God, just as it is not merely difficult
but impossible for a camel to pass through the eye of a needle –
even a needle of the largest size. The listeners were dismayed:
'Then who can be saved?' they asked. (Being saved in the

Gospels is a further synonym for entering the kingdom of God and inheriting eternal life.) The disciples themselves were not affluent: Peter spoke for the others when he said, 'we have left everything and followed you' (Mark 10:28). But they had not realised, perhaps, just how stringent the terms of entry into the kingdom were – and are.

Not only those who heard the words when they were first spoken, but many others since, have found the saying to be a hard one. Attempts have been made to soften it somewhat. The eye of a needle, we are sometimes assured, is a metaphor: the reference is to a small opening giving independent access or egress through a much larger city gate. Visitors are sometimes shown such a small entrance in one of the city gates of Jerusalem or another Eastern city and are told that this is what Jesus had in mind. If a man approaches the city gate on camel-back when it is closed, he can dismount and get through the small entrance on foot, but there is no way for a camel to do so, especially if it is loaded: it must wait for the main gate to be opened to let it through. Even if a small camel, unloaded, tried to get through the small entrance, it would be in danger of sticking half-way. It is ordinarily impossible for a camel to get through such a narrow opening, but not so ludicrously impossible as for anyone to try to get it through the eye of a needle. But this charming explanation is of relatively recent date: there is no evidence that such a subsidiary entrance was called the eye of a needle in biblical times.

Others point out that there is a Greek word (*kamilos*) meaning 'cable' very similar in appearance and sound to the word (*kamēlos*) meaning 'camel'. In fact the word meaning 'cable' appears in a few late witnesses to the gospel text. Their reading is reflected in a version of the English New Testament entitled *The Book of Books*, issued in 1938 to mark the quatercentenary of Henry VIII's injunction requiring a copy of the English Bible to be placed in every parish church in England: 'It is easier for a rope to go through the eye of a needle than for a rich man to enter the kingdom of God'. The editors of *The Book of Books* did not commit themselves to the view that the word meaning 'rope' or 'cable' stood in the original text: they simply remarked that while the familiar form with 'camel' would 'doubtless be preferred by Eastern readers', their own chosen reading 'makes a more vivid appeal to the West'. This is doubtful. In any case, the substitution of 'cable' or 'rope' for 'camel' should probably be recognised as 'an attempt to soften the rigour of the statement'.[1] 'To contrast the largest beast of burden known in Palestine with the smallest of artificial apertures is quite in the manner of Christ's proverbial sayings.'[2] In Jewish rabbinical literature an *elephant* passing through the eye of a needle is a figure of speech for sheer impossibility.[3]

No doubt Jesus was using the language of hyperbole, as when he spoke of the man with a whole plank sticking out of his eye offering to remove the splinter or speck of sawdust from his neighbour's eye (Matt. 7:3–5; Luke 6:41–42). But the language of hyperbole was intended to drive the lesson home: it is impossible for a rich man to enter the kingdom of God – humanly impossible, Jesus concedes, for God, with whom nothing is impossible, can even save a rich man. But if so, then the rich man's heart must be changed, by having its attachment to material riches replaced by attachment to the true riches, 'treasure in heaven'.

It is not easy for anyone to enter the kingdom of God – 'the gate is narrow and the way is hard' (Matt. 7:14) – but it is most difficult of all for the rich. Jesus's absolute statement in Mark 10:24, 'how hard it is to enter the kingdom of God!' has been expanded in later witnesses to the text so as to read: 'how hard it is *for those who trust in riches* to enter the kingdom of God!' This could be another attempt to soften the hardness of his words, making it possible for a reader to comfort himself with the thought: 'I have riches, indeed, but I do not trust in them: I am all right.' But, according to Jesus's teaching, it was very difficult for people who had riches not to trust in them. They would show whether they trusted in riches or not by their readiness to part with them. But the inserted words, 'for those who trust in riches', are not so wide of the mark. What was it about riches that made Jesus regard them as an obstacle to entrance into the kingdom? Simply the fact that those who had them relied on them, like the rich farmer in the parable (Luke

12:16–21; see p. 185), who encouraged himself with the thought of the great wealth which he had stored up for a long time to come, or his counterpart today whose investments are bringing in a comfortable, inflation-proof income.

There is probably no saying of Jesus which is 'harder' in the Western mind today than the saying about the camel and the needle's eye, none which carries with it such a strong temptation to tone it down.

49

SERVING GOD AND MAMMON

'You cannot serve God and mammon' (Matt. 6:24;
Luke 16:13)

'Mammon' is a term that Jesus sometimes used to denote
wealth. He was not the only teacher in Israel to use it, and
whenever it is used it seems to indicate some unworthy aspect
of wealth – not so much, perhaps, the unworthiness of wealth
itself as the unworthiness of many people's attitudes to it. The
derivation of the word is uncertain. Some think that it
originally meant that in which men and women put their trust;
others, that it originally meant 'accumulation', 'piling up'. But
the derivation is not very important; it is the use of a word, not
its derivation, that determines its meaning.

Since the service of mammon is presented in this saying as an
alternative to the service of God, mammon seems to be a rival
to God. Service of mammon and service of God are mutually
exclusive. The servant of mammon, in other words, is an idol-
worshipper: mammon, wealth, money has become his idol, the
object of his worship.

The man who depended on finding enough work today to
buy the next day's food for his family could pray with feeling,
'Give us this day our daily bread' (Matt. 6:11) or, as Moffat
rendered it, 'give us to-day our bread for the morrow'. But the
man who knew he had enough laid by to maintain his family
and himself, whether he worked or not, whether he kept well or
fell ill, would not put the same urgency into the prayer. The
more material resources he had, the less whole-hearted his

reliance on God would tend to become. The children of the kingdom, in Jesus's teaching, are marked by their instant and constant trust in God; that trust will be weakened if they have something else to trust in.

In the Western world today we are cushioned, by social security and the like, against the uncertainties and hardships of life in a way that was not contemplated in New Testament times. It was in a society that did not provide widows' pensions that the words of 1 Tim. 5:5 were written: 'She who is a real widow, and is left all alone, has set her hope on God and continues in supplications and prayers night and day.' This is not a criticism of social security (for which God be thanked); it is a reminder of the difficulty we find in applying the sayings of Jesus and his apostles to our own condition. But when we view the starving Karamajong in Uganda, or the uprooted Boat People of Vietnam, we can try to imagine what it must be like to be in their situation, and consider what claim they have on our resources. This will not get us into the kingdom of God, but at least it may teach us to use material property more worthily than by treating it as something to lay our hearts on or rest our confidence in.

A covetous person, says Paul, is an idolater (Eph. 5:5), and in saying so he expressed the same idea as Jesus did when he spoke about mammon. 'Take heed, and beware of all covetousness,' said Jesus on another occasion, 'for a man's life does not consist in the abundance of his possessions' (Luke 12:15). That should teach us not to say 'How much is So-and-so worth?' when we really mean 'How much does he possess?' Luke follows this last saying with the parable of the rich fool, the man who had so much property that he reckoned he could take life easy for a long time to come. He went to bed with this comforting thought, but by morning he was a pauper – he was dead, and had to leave his property behind. He had treated it as mammon, the object of his ultimate concern, and in his hour of greatest need it proved useless to him. If he had put his trust in God and accumulated the true and lasting riches, he would not have found himself destitute after death.

50.

USING UNRIGHTEOUS MAMMON TO MAKE FRIENDS

'And I tell you, make friends for yourselves by means of unrighteousness mammon, so that when it fails they may receive you into the eternal habitations' (Luke 16:9)

This is the 'moral' of the parable of the dishonest steward, a story which presents problems of its own. The steward looked after his master's estate, dealt with the other employees and tenants, and in general should have relieved his master of all concern about the day-to-day running of his affairs. But he mismanaged the estate, and not simply (it appears) through incompetence or negligence, until the time came when his master discovered that his affairs were in bad shape and ordered the steward to turn in his books, since his employment was terminated.

Before he turned in his books, the steward took some hasty measures with an eye to his future interests. In particular, he summoned his master's debtors and reduced their debts substantially, altering the entries accordingly. Perhaps we are to understand that he made good the difference out of his own pocket: if he did, his money was well invested. He wanted to be sure of bed and board when he was dismissed from his employment with no severance benefit. No one would take him on as steward (his master was not likely to give him the kind of testimonial that would encourage any other landowner to employ him); the alternatives were casual labour (digging, for example) or begging. He did not feel strong enough for the former, and to be a beggar would be insufferably disgraceful. But if he made some friends now by a judicious expenditure of his means, they might give him shelter when he was evicted from his tied cottage.

His master got to know of his action and called him a clever rascal. No more than this need be understood of Jesus's remark that 'The master commended the dishonest steward for his prudence' (Luke 16:8). The master may well have recognised some analogy between the steward's conduct and the methods by which his own wealth had been amassed. 'You see,' said Jesus, 'worldly people, with no thoughts beyond this present life, will sometimes behave more sensibly and providently than other-worldly people, "the children of light". *They* will use material wealth to prepare for their earthly future; why cannot the children of light use it to prepare for their eternal future? Use the "unrighteous mammon" to win yourselves friends in the world to come.' It is called 'unrighteous mammon' because it is too often acquired unjustly and used for unjust ends. It is ethically neutral in itself; it is people's attitudes to it and ways of dealing with it that are reprehensible. As has often been pointed out, it is not money as such but 'the love of money' which scripture affirms to be 'the root of all evils' (1 Tim. 6:10).

But how can material wealth be used to procure friends who will receive one 'into the eternal habitations' when it is no longer accessible? This parable is followed by a collection of isolated sayings several of which are concerned with the subject of wealth, and then comes another story – the story of the rich man and Lazarus. In it we meet a man who had plenty of the 'unrighteous mammon' and used it all to secure comfort and good cheer for himself in this life, giving no thought to the life to come. The time came when he would have been very glad to have even one friend to welcome him into the 'eternal habitations', but he found none. Yet he had every opportunity of securing such a friend. There at his gate lay Lazarus, destitute and covered with sores, only too glad to catch and eat the pieces of bread which the rich man and his guests used to wipe their fingers at table and then threw to the dogs outside. If the rich man had used a little of his wealth to help Lazarus, he would have had a friend to speak up for him on the other side. 'This man', Lazarus might have said to Abraham, 'showed me the kindness of God on earth.' But Lazarus had been given no ground to say any such thing. The rich man in Hades found himself without a friend when he needed one most – and he had no one to blame but himself.

51.

THE GREAT GULF

'Between us and you a great chasm has been fixed, in order that those who would pass from here to you may not be able, and none may cross from there to us' (Luke 16:26)

These words are part of Abraham's reply to the rich man, explaining why Lazarus could not go and cool his tongue with a drop of water and so relieve his anguish.

In view of what has been said about the rich man's failure to make friends by means of his wealth, there may be a problem here. Even if he had used some of his wealth to help Lazarus on earth, and Lazarus had therefore been willing to do something for him in the afterworld, how could Lazarus have crossed the great gulf or chasm that lay between them? But the chasm is not a geographical one, whose width and depth could be measured. When the story is read nowadays in the AV, a wrong impression may be given by the statement that, when the rich man died and was buried, 'in hell he lift up his eyes, being in torments' (Luke 16:23). As our more recent versions indicate, 'hell' means Hades, the undifferentiated abode of the dead. It was not because he was in Hades that the rich man was in pain, but because of his past life. Had he made a friend of Lazarus by helping him in his wretchedness, there would not have been the impassable gulf which prevented Lazarus from coming to help him. The impassable gulf, in fact, was of the rich man's own creating. This may mean more or less what C. S. Lewis expressed by a different metaphor when he suggested that 'the doors of hell' (and he meant the abode of the damned, not just the abode of the dead) 'are locked on the *inside*'.[1]

The story of the rich man and Lazarus appears to have a literary and oral prehistory, and it is interesting to explore this. But such exploration will not help us much to understand it in the context which Luke has given it (and Luke is the only evangelist to record it).

The rich man, hearing that it is impossible for Lazarus to come and help him, turns his mind to something else. Let Lazarus be sent back to earth to warn the rich man's five brothers to mend their ways, lest they find themselves after death sharing his own sad lot. Perhaps there is the implication here: 'If only someone had come back to warn me, I should not have found myself in this plight.' But Abraham replies that they have all the warning they need: 'They have Moses and the prophets', that is, the Bible. If the rich man himself had paid heed to what Moses and the prophets say about the blessedness of those who consider the poor – a theme so pervasive that it cannot well be overlooked – it would have been better for him.

But Moses and the prophets are not enough, argued the rich man. Let them have an exceptional sign that will compel their repentance. Abraham's response has special relevance to what was happening in the course of Jesus's ministry. People asked him to validate his claim that the kingdom of God had approached them in his ministry by showing them a sign from heaven – something spectacular that would compel them to acknowledge his authority to speak and act as he did. He refused to grant their request: if his works and words were not self-authenticating, then no external sign, however impressive, could be any more persuasive (see p. 96). Moses and the prophets, pleads the rich man, are not persuasive enough, 'but if some one goes to them from the dead, they will repent'. But Abraham has the last word: 'If they do not hear Moses and the prophets, neither will they be convinced if some one should rise from the dead' (Luke 16:31). Or, as James Denney paraphrased it, 'If they can be inhuman with the Bible in their hands and Lazarus at their gate, no revelation of the splendours of heaven or the anguish of hell will ever make them anything else.'[2]

Is it a pure coincidence that another of the evangelists tells of a Lazarus who did come back from the dead? His restoration to life was certainly a very impressive sign, which strengthened the faith of those who already believed in Jesus, or were disposed to believe in him, but according to John it strengthened the determination of those who were convinced that the safety of the nation demanded Jesus's death – indeed, they 'planned to put Lazarus also to death, because on account of him many of the Jews were going away and believing in Jesus' (John 12:10–11).

But by the time Luke wrote his Gospel a greater than Lazarus had risen from the dead. The proclamation that Christ had been raised 'in accordance with the scriptures' (1 Cor. 15:4) led many to believe in him, but it did not compel belief; even his resurrection did not convince those who had made up their minds not to believe.

52.

WILL THE SON OF MAN FIND FAITH ON EARTH?

'Nevertheless, when the Son of man comes, will he find faith on earth?' (Luke 18:8).

This is a hard saying in the sense that no one can be quite sure what it means, especially in relation to its context. When a question is asked in Greek, it is often possible to determine, from the presence of one particle or another, whether the answer expected is 'Yes' or 'No'. But no such help is given with this one. Many commentators assume that the answer implied here is 'No', but in form at least it is a completely open question.

Luke is the only evangelist who records the question, and he places it at the end of the parable of the persistent widow – the widow who refused to take 'No' for an answer. Jesus told this parable, says Luke, to teach his disciples that 'they ought always to pray and not lose heart' (Luke 18:1). But what has this purpose to do with the Son of man's finding faith on earth when he comes?

The widow in the parable showed faith of an unusually persevering quality – not personal faith in the unjust judge whom she pestered until he granted her petition to keep her quiet, but faith in the efficacy of persistent 'prayer'. The point of the story seems to be this: if even a conscienceless judge, who 'neither fears God nor regards man', sees to it that a widow gets her rights, not for the sake of seeing justice done but to get rest from her importunity, how much more will God, who is no unjust judge but a loving Father, listen to his children's plea for vindication! It is vindication that they seek, just as the widow insisted on getting her rights, of which someone was trying to deprive her.

Then comes the question: 'when the Son of man comes, will he find faith on earth?' It is possible indeed that it is Luke who attaches the question to the parable, and that in Jesus's teaching it had some other context which is no longer recoverable. T. W. Manson leant to the view that 'the Son of man' does not bear its special meaning here – that the sense is: 'Men and women ought to have implicit faith that God will vindicate his elect people, that righteousness will triumph over evil. But when one comes and looks for such faith – when, for example, I come and look for it – is it anywhere to be found?' The answer implied by this interpretation is 'No' – people in general, it is suggested, do not really expect God to vindicate his chosen ones, nor do they at heart desire the triumph of righteousness over evil.[1]

But perhaps we should look at a wider context than this one parable. The coming of the Son of man is a major theme in the preceding section of Luke's record, in the discourse of Jesus about 'the day when the Son of man is revealed' (Luke 17:22–37). The lesson impressed by this discourse on the hearers is that they must keep on the alert and be ready for that day when it comes. When it comes, God will vindicate his righteous cause, and therewith the cause of his people who trust in him. But they must trust him and not lose heart; they must here and now continue faithfully in the work assigned to them. (This is the lesson also of the parable of the pounds in Luke 19:11–27.) The Son of man, whose revelation will be like the lightning, illuminating 'the sky from one side to the other' (Luke 17:24), will be able to survey the earth to see if there is any faith on it, any 'faithful and wise steward' whom his master when he comes will find loyally fulfilling his service (Luke 12:42–44).

So the question 'will he find faith on earth?' remains an open one in fact as it is in form: its answer depends on the faithful obedience of those who wait to render an account of their stewardship when he calls for it.

53.

THE RATE FOR THE JOB?

'Take what belongs to you, and go; I choose to give to this last as I give to you. Am I not allowed to do what I choose with what belongs to me? Or do you begrudge me my generosity?' (Matt. 20:14–15).

One of the complaints that right-living and religious people made about Jesus arose from his treatment of the more disreputable members of society. They might have agreed that such persons should not be entirely excluded from the mercy of the all-loving God. Even for them there was hope, if they showed that they were not beyond redemption by practical repentance and unquestionable amendment of life. But not until such evidence had been given could they begin to be accepted as friends and neighbours.

Jesus, however, accepted them immediately; he did not wait to see the outcome before he committed himself to them. This was disturbing; it was even more disturbing that he seemed to think more highly of them than of those who had never blotted their public copy-book. He gave the impression that he actually preferred the company of the rejects of society: he not only made them feel at home in his company, so that they felt free to take liberties with him that they would never have thought of taking with an ordinary rabbi, but he even accepted invitations to share a meal with them and appeared genuinely to enjoy such an occasion. When he was challenged for this unconventional behaviour, his reply was that this was how

God treated sinners; and he told several parables to reinforce this lesson.

One of these parables tells of the man who hired a number of casual labourers to gather the grapes in his vineyard when the appropriate time of year came round. It is a disconcerting parable on more levels than one. A highly respected trade union leader of our day is said to feel very unhappy when he is asked to read this parable as a scripture lesson in church, because it seems to defend the unacceptable principle of equal pay for unequal work.

There are certain seasons when a farmer or a vine-grower requires a large supply of labour for a short period. Until recently the autumn mid-term school holiday was known in Scotland as the 'potato-lifting' holiday, because it fell at the right time to release an ample supply of cheap juvenile assistance for gathering the potatoes from the fields. In the economic depression from which most of Palestine suffered in the time of Jesus anyone who wanted a short-term supply of labour for this kind of purpose was sure of finding it. The vine-grower in the parable had only to go to the market-place of the village and there he would find a number of unemployed men hanging around in hope that someone would come and offer them a job.

At daybreak, then, this vine-grower went to the market-place and hired several men to do a day's work for him gathering grapes. The agreed rate for such a day's work was a denarius, which was evidently sufficient to keep a labourer and his family at subsistence level for a day. Apparently the vine-grower wanted the job completed within one day. As he considered the amount of work to be done and the speed at which the men were working, he decided that he would need more hands, so at three-hourly intervals he went and hired more. He did not bargain with them for a denarius or part of a denarius: he promised to give them what was proper. Then, just an hour before sunset, in order to ensure that the work would not be left unfinished, he went back and found a few men still unemployed, so he sent them to join the others working in the vineyard.

An hour later the work was finished, and the workers queued up to receive their pay, the last-hired being at the head of the queue. They had no idea what they would get for an hour's work; in fact, each of them received a denarius. So did the men who had worked three hours, six hours and nine hours. At last came those who had been hired at daybreak and had done twelve hours' work: what would they get? Each of them similarly got a denarius. They complained, 'Why should these others get as much as we have done? Why should not we get more after a hard day's work?' But the vine-grower told them that they had no cause for complaint. They had agreed to do a day's work for a denarius, and he had kept his promise to give them that. It was no business of theirs what he gave to others who had entered into no agreement with him for a fixed sum. He might have said, 'They and their families have to live.' But he did not: he simply said, 'Can't I do what I like with my own money?'

The law-abiding people whom Jesus knew tended to feel that they had made a bargain with God: if they kept his commandments, he would give them the blessings promised to those who did so. They would have no reason to complain if God treated them fairly and kept his promises. But what about those others who had broken his commandments, who had started to do his will late in the day after their encounter with Jesus and the way of the kingdom? They were in no position to strike a bargain with God: they could do nothing but cast themselves on his grace, like the tax-collector in another parable who could only say, 'God have mercy on me, sinner that I am!' (Luke 18:13). What could they expect? The lesson of the parable seems to be this: when people make a bargain with God, he will honour his promise and give them no cause for complaint; but there is no limit to what his grace will do for those who have no claim at all on him but trust entirely to his goodness. If it be said that this gives them an unfair advantage, let it be considered that they were terribly disadvantaged to begin with. If it be urged that their rehabilitation should involve some payment for their past misdeeds, the truth may be that they have paid enough already. Should those who have turned to God at the eleventh hour and given him only the last twelfth of life get as much of heaven as those who have given him a whole lifetime? If God is pleased to give them as much, who will tell him that he should not? If God did not delight in mercy, it would go hard with the best of us:

> Though justice by thy plea, consider this,
> That, in the course of justice, none of us
> Should see salvation.[1]

The first arrivals might not have complained if the last comers had been paid only a small fraction of what they themselves received. There was in fact, as T. W. Manson points out in his treatment of this parable, a coin worth one-twelfth of a denarius: 'It was called a *pondion*. But there is no such thing as a twelfth part of the love of God.'[2]

54.

THE FIRST WILL BE LAST

'But many that are first will be last, and the last first'
(Mark 10:31; Matt. 19:30; cf. Luke 13:30; Matt. 20:16).

The saying about the first being last and the last first is not
peculiar to the teaching of Jesus; it is a piece of general folk
wisdom, which finds memorable expression in Aesop's fable of
the hare and the tortoise. But in the Gospels it is applied to the
living situation during Jesus's ministry.

The saying occurs in two contexts in the Gospels. The first
context (in Mark 10:31 and the parallel in Matthew 19:30) is
the sequel to the incident of the rich man who could not bring
himself to sell his property and give the proceeds to the poor.
Jesus commented on the difficulty experienced by any rich
man who tried to get into the kingdom of God, and Peter spoke
up: 'Well, we at least are not rich; we have given up everything
to be your followers' (see pp. 180–3). To this Jesus replied
that, even in this age, those who had given up anything for him
would receive more than ample compensation, over and above
the persecutions which would inevitably fall to the lot of his
followers, while in the age to come they would receive eternal
life. Then he added, 'But many that are first will be last, and the
last first.'

What is the point of the saying in this context? It seems to be
directed to the disciples, and perhaps the point is that those
who have given up most to follow Jesus must not suppose that
the chief place in the kingdom of God is thereby guaranteed to
them. It is possible to take pride in one's self-denial and

suppose that by its means one has established a special claim on God. 'No amount of exertion, not even self-denial or asceticism, can make one a disciple. Discipleship is purely a gift of God.'[1] Even those who have made great sacrifices for God are not justified in his sight for that reason; and even Peter and his companions, who gave up all to follow Jesus, may get a surprise on the day of review and reward by seeing others receiving preference over them.

In Luke 13:30 the words (but in the reverse order: 'some are last who will be first, and some are first who will be last') are added to Jesus's affirmation that 'men will come from east and west, and from north and south, and sit at table in the kingdom of God' (in Matthew 8:11 this affirmation is attached to the incident of the centurion's servant). Those who come from the four points of the compass are plainly Gentiles, whereas some of Jesus's Jewish hearers, who looked forward confidently to a place in the kingdom, along with 'Abraham and Isaac and Jacob and all the prophets', would find themselves shut out. The free offer of the gospel might be extended 'to the Jew first' (Rom. 1:16), but if those to whom it was first extended paid no heed to it, then the Gentiles, late starters though they were, would receive its blessings first (see p. 105).

In Matthew 20:16 the parable of the labourers in the vineyard (see p. 196) is rounded off with these words: 'So the last will be first, and the first last.' In the parable the last-hired workmen received the same wage at the end of the day as those who were hired at dawn. It might be said indeed that in that situation there was neither first nor last: all were treated equally. But the words had a wider fulfilment in Jesus's ministry. Those who were far ahead in understanding and practice of the law found themselves falling behind those whom they despised in receiving the good things of the kingdom of God. The son who said 'I will' to his father's command but did nothing about it naturally yielded precedence to the son who, having first said 'I will not', later repented and did it. Similarly, said Jesus to the chief priests and elders in Jerusalem, 'the tax collectors and the harlots go into the kingdom of God before you' (Matt. 21:28–32). This was a hard saying to those who heard it, who must indeed have regarded it as an insult – as many of their present-day counterparts equally would. But the work of Jesus brings about many reversals, and the day of judgment will be full of surprises.

55.

MANY ARE CALLED,
BUT FEW ARE CHOSEN

'For many are called, but few are chosen' (Matt. 22:14).

In the original text of the Gospels, these words appear once – as a comment on Matthew's parable of the marriage feast. In the course of transmission of the text it came to be attached to the parable of the labourers in the vineyard also (Matt. 20:16), where it appears, for example, in the AV, but it is not really relevant there.

In form this seems to be a proverbial saying; other sayings with the same construction are found elsewhere in ancient literature. Plato quotes one with reference to the mystery religions: 'many are the wand-bearers, but few are the initiates'[1]; that is to say, there are many who walk in the procession to the cult-centre carrying sacred wands, but only a few are admitted to the knowledge of the innermost secret (which confers the prize of immortality). Two sayings with this construction are ascribed to Jesus or his disciples in the second-century *Gospel of Thomas*. In Saying 74 one of the disciples says to him, 'Lord, there are many around the opening but no one in the well.' (The well is the well of truth: many approach it without getting into it. In this form the saying has a gnostic flavour; in fact, Celsus, an anti-Christian writer of the second century, quotes it from a gnostic treatise called the *Heavenly Dialogue*.[2]) Jesus's reply to the disciple is given in Saying 75: 'Many stand outside at the door, but it is only the single ones who enter the bridal chamber.' (In gnostic terminology the bridal chamber is the place where the soul is reunited with its proper element and the 'single ones' are those who have transcended the distinctions of age and sex. Hence Saying 49 makes Jesus say, 'Happy are the single and the chosen ones, for you will find the kingdom.')

The gnostic ideas of the *Gospel of Thomas* will give us no help in understanding the saying as it appears at the end of the parable of the wedding feast. There the 'called' are those who were invited to the wedding feast; the 'chosen' are those who accepted the invitation. The king invited many guests to the feast, but only a few, if any, of those who were invited actually came to it. The feast is a parable of the gospel and the blessings which it holds out to believers. The invitation to believe the gospel and enjoy its blessings goes out to all who hear it. But if all receive the call, not all respond to it. Those who do respond show by that very fact they are 'chosen'. Protestant theologians used to distinguish between the 'common call', addressed to all who hear the gospel, and the 'effectual call', received by those who actually respond. In part 2 of Bunyan's *Pilgrim's Progress* Christiana and her family are taught this lesson in the Interpreter's house by means of a hen and her chickens: 'She had a common call, and that she hath all day long. She had a special call, and that she had but sometimes.' The only way in which the effectual call can be distinguished from the common call is that those who hear it respond to it. 'Effectual calling is the work of God's Spirit, whereby, convincing us of our sin and misery, enlightening our minds in the knowledge of Christ, and renewing our wills, he doth persuade and enable us to embrace Jesus Christ, freely offered to us in the gospel.'[3]

Paul insists that 'it is not the hearers of the law who are righteous before God, but the doers of the law who will be justified' (Rom. 2:13), and it is those who live 'according to the Spirit' in whom 'the just requirement of the law' is fulfilled. James, to the same effect, urges his readers to 'be doers of the word, and not hearers only' (James 1:22).

The gnostic teachers whose ideas are reflected in the *Gospel of Thomas* rather liked the idea that 'the single and the chosen ones' were a small minority, provided they themselves were included in that élite number. On one occasion the disciples tried to make Jesus commit himself on the relative number of the called and the chosen, asking, 'Lord, will those who are saved be few?' (Luke 13:23). But he refused to gratify their curiosity: he simply told them to make sure that they themselves entered in through the narrow gate, 'for many, I tell you, will seek to enter and will not be able.'

It has frequently been taken for granted that Jesus's words about the relative fewness of the saved had reference not only to the period of his ministry but to all time. William Fisher, elder of the parish of Mauchline, Ayrshire, in the later part of the eighteeenth century, estimated the proportion as one to ten; but that may have been a piece of speculation on the part of a man who, convinced that he himself was one of the chosen, preferred to keep the number small and select. In any case, his estimate has been immortalised by the national poet of Scotland.[4] More recently, and more seriously, Mr. Enoch Powell has interpreted Jesus's words, 'few are chosen', as an assertion 'that his salvation will not be for all, not even for the majority', and has insisted that 'ignorance, incapacity, perversity, the sheer human propensity to error are sufficient to ensure a high failure rate'.[5] They are sufficient, indeed, to ensure a hundred-per-cent failure rate, but for the grace of God. But when divine grace begins to operate, the situation is transformed.

It may well be that Jesus was speaking more particularly of the situation during his ministry when he spoke of the few and the many. Even the casual reader of the New Testament gathers that there was a great and rapid increase in the number of his followers after his death and resurrection. Within a few months from his crucifixion, the number of his followers in Palestine was ten times as great as it had been during his ministry. And Paul, the greatest theologian of primitive Christianity, speaks of those who receive the saving benefit of the work of Jesus as 'the many' (Rom. 5:15, 19). No reasonable interpretation can make 'the many' mean a minority for, as John Calvin put it in his commentary on those words of Paul, 'if Adam's fall had the effect of producing the ruin of many, the grace of God is much more efficacious in benefiting many, since admittedly Christ is much more powerful to save than Adam was to ruin.'[6]

56.

THE WEDDING GARMENT

'"Friend, how did you get in here without a wedding garment?"' (Matt. 22:12)

The incident of the man who had no wedding garment is attached in Matthew's Gospel to the parable of the wedding feast (Matt. 22:1–10). The parable of the wedding feast has a parallel in the parable of the great banquet in Luke 14:16–24. There are differences of detail between the two parables, but the main outline of the story is the same: the host (a king, in Matthew's version) invites many guests, but on the day of the feast they excuse themselves for various reasons. But all the preparations have been made: the food (and plenty of it) is waiting to be eaten. The host therefore sends his servants out into the streets and lanes to round up those whom they find there and bring them to the banqueting hall. All the empty places are filled, and filled by people who are only too glad to be set down face to face with a square meal. They do full justice to what has been provided, even if those who were originally invited are not interested.

This is readily understood as a parable of Jesus's proclamation of the kingdom of God. The religious people, those who attended synagogue regularly, were not really interested in what he had to say and despised the good news which he brought. But the outcasts of society recognised his message as just what they had been waiting for. The blessings of the gospel, the Father's loving forgiveness, exactly suited their need and they eagerly seized what Jesus had to give.

But the wedding garment presents a problem. How could people who had been swept in from the streets be expected to have suitable clothes for a festive occasion? One man was asked how he got in without a wedding garment, but they might all have been expected to be similarly unprovided with suitable attire. It would have been more surprising if one of them had come in actually wearing a wedding garment. It may be suggested that the royal host thoughtfully provided them with suitable clothes, but this is not said in the parable, and the implication is that the man who was improperly dressed could have come properly clad. When taxed with his failure he had no excuse: he was 'speechless'.

It is most probable that this was originally a separate parable. If the host was a king, he would expect those whom he invited to a banquet to honour him by coming appropriately dressed: failure in this respect would be a studied insult to him. The culprit in this case might count himself fortunate if nothing worse befell him than to be trussed up and thrown out into the darkness, to grind his teeth in annoyance with himself for having been so foolish. The requirement of a wedding garment, unsuitable for people peremptorily conscripted from the streets to come and enjoy a free supper, was eminently suitable for the guests whom a king or magnate would normally invite to dine with him. What then is the point of the garment in the parable, if it was originally a parable on its own? Clothes are not infrequently used in the Bible as a symbol of personal character, and it is possibly implied that some might think themselves entitled to be counted among the 'children of the kingdom' or the followers of Jesus whose character was out of keeping with such a profession. If so, then the parable of the wedding garment would be a warning against false discipleship: it is not saying 'Lord, lord' that admits one to the kingdom, but doing the heavenly Father's will (Matt. 7:21).

57.

THE CURSING OF THE FIG TREE

'May no one ever eat fruit from you again' (Mark 11:14)

This incident is related by Mark and, in a more compressed form, by Matthew. According to Mark, Jesus and his disciples spent the night following his entry into Jerusalem in Bethany. Next morning they returned to Jerusalem. On the way he felt hungry, 'and seeing in the distance a fig tree in leaf, he went to see if he could find anything on it. When he came to it, he found nothing but leaves, for it was not the season for figs.' Then come the words quoted above. They continued on their way into Jerusalem, where that day he cleansed the temple; in the evening they returned to Bethany. Next morning, as they passed the same place, they saw the fig tree withered away to its roots. And Peter remembered and said to him, 'Rabbi, look! The fig tree which you cursed has withered' (Mark 11:20-21).

Was it not unreasonable to curse the tree for being fruitless when, as Mark expressly says, 'it was not the season for figs'? The problem is most satisfactorily cleared up in a discussion of 'The Barren Fig Tree' published many years ago by W. M. Christie, a Church of Scotland minister in Palestine under the British mandatory regime. He pointed out first the time of year at which the incident is said to have occurred (if, as is probable, Jesus was crucified on April 6th, A.D. 30, the incident occurred during the first days of April). 'Now,' wrote Dr. Christie, 'the facts connected with the fig tree are these. Towards the end of March the leaves begin to appear, and in about a week the foliage coating is complete. Coincident with [this], and sometimes even before, there appears quite a crop of small knobs, not the real figs, but a kind of early forerunner. They grow to the size of green almonds, in which condition they are eaten by peasants and others when hungry. When they come to their own indefinite maturity they drop off.'[1] These precursors of the true fig are called *taqsh* in Palestinian Arabic. Their appearance is a harbinger of the fully formed appearance of the true fig some six weeks later. So, as Mark says, the time for figs had not yet come. But if the leaves appear without any *taqsh*, that is a sign that there will be no figs. Since Jesus found 'nothing but leaves' – leaves without any *taqsh* – he knew that 'it was an absolutely hopeless, fruitless fig tree', and said as much.

But if that is the true explanation of his words, why should anyone trouble to record the incident as though it had some special significance? Because it did have some special significance. As recorded by Mark, it is an acted parable with the same lesson as the spoken parable of the fruitless fig tree in Luke 13:6–9. In that spoken parable a landowner came three years in succession expecting fruit from a fig tree on his property, and when year by year it proved to be fruitless, he told the man in charge of his vineyard to cut it down because it was using up the ground to no good purpose. In both the acted parable and the spoken parable it is difficult to avoid the conclusion that the fig tree represents the city of Jerusalem, unresponsive to Jesus as he came to it with the message of God, and thereby incurring destruction. Elsewhere Luke records how Jesus wept over the city's blindness to its true well-being and foretold its ruin 'because you did not know the time of your visitation' (Luke 19:41–44). It is because the incident of the cursing of the fig tree was seen to convey the same lesson that Mark, followed by Matthew, recorded it.

58.

FAITH THAT REMOVES MOUNTAINS

'Truly, I say to you, whoever says to this mountain, "Be taken up and cast into the sea", and does not doubt in his heart, but believes that what he says will come to pass, it will be done for him' (Mark 11:23)

'If you had faith as a grain of mustard seed, you could say to this sycamine tree, "Be rooted up, and be planted in the sea", and it would obey you' (Luke 17:6)

'For truly, I say to you, if you have faith as a grain of mustard seed, you will say to this mountain, "Move hence to yonder place", and it will move; and nothing will be impossible to you' (Matt. 17:20)

Of these sayings, or varieties of an original saying, emphasising the limitless possibilities open to faith, Mark's form (followed in Matthew 21:21) has a life-setting in the neighbourhood of Jerusalem, during Holy Week; Luke's form may be from the Q collection, in which case the form in Matthew 17:20 (an amplification of Jesus's words to the disciples after the healing of the epileptic boy at the foot of the mountain of transfiguration) combines features from Mark and Q.

In any case, Jesus illustrates the power of faith by analogies from the natural world. If faith is present at all, even if it is no bigger than a mustard seed, it can accomplish wonders: think what a large plant springs from something as tiny as a mustard seed. 'We are not afraid when the earth heaves and the mountains are hurled into the sea': so Psalm 46:2 (NEB) describes a real or figurative convulsion of nature which leaves

men and women of God unshaken because he is their refuge
and strength. It may be that Jesus is using such a form of words
figuratively to describe the incalculable effects of prevailing
faith.

But in Mark's account there may be some more explicit
point in the form of words. In that account the words are
addressed to the disciples after the incident of the cursing of the
fig tree. There may not seem to be much to connect that
incident with a lesson on the power of faith. The connection,
however, may be provided by the place where, according to
Mark, the words were spoken. They were spoken in the
morning, as Jesus and his disciples made their way from
Bethany to Jerusalem, crossing the Mount of Olives. So, in
Mark's account, 'this mountain' in the saying would be the
Mount of Olives.

Now, in current expectation regarding the time of the end,
the Mount of Olives played a special part. It would be the scene
of a violent earthquake on the Day of the Lord. 'On that day',
said one of the prophets (referring to the day when the God of
Israel would take final action against the enemies of his
people), 'his feet shall stand on the Mount of Olives which lies
before Jerusalem on the east; and the Mount of Olives shall be
split in two from east to west by a very wide valley; so that one
half of the Mount shall withdraw northward, and the other half
southward' (Zech. 14:4). If Jesus had this and related Old
Testament prophecies in mind on his way across the Mount of
Olives, his meaning might have been, 'If you have sufficient
faith in God, the Day of the Lord will come sooner than you
think.' (For this suggestion indebtedness should be acknowledged to a work by Professor William Manson, published in
1943.[1])

59

NEITHER WILL I TELL YOU

'Neither will I tell you by what authority I do these things' (Mark 11:33; Matt. 21:27; Luke 20:8)

Why did Jesus refuse to give a straight answer to those who asked him why he acted as he did?

It was during Holy Week, while he was walking in the temple precincts in Jerusalem, that some representatives of the Sanhedrin, Israel's supreme court (comprising chief priests, scribes and elders, as Mark tells us in verse 27), came to Jesus and asked him, 'By what authority are you doing these things, or who gave you this authority to do them?' By 'these things' they meant not so much his teaching in the outer court but his cleansing of the temple, which had taken place the previous day. What right had he to put a stop to buying and selling within the bounds of the temple, or to forbid 'any one to carry anything through the temple' – to use the outer court as a short cut on their business errands? Many religious people might have agreed with him that the sacred area should not be turned into a bazaar, but a temple police force was stationed to protect its sanctity: who authorised Jesus to act as he did?

His cleansing of the temple was what would have been recognised in Old Testament times as a prophetic action – the kind of action by which a prophet would occasionally confirm his spoken message and bring it home to the people around him. Jesus protested that the temple was being prevented from fulfilling its purpose as 'a house of prayer for all the nations' (cf. Isa. 56:7). Gentiles were not allowed to enter the inner courts, but in the outer court they might draw near to the true and living God and worship him, like those 'Greeks' who, according to John 12:20, went up to worship at Passover. Because of this the outer court was sometimes called 'the court of the Gentiles'. But Gentiles were hindered in using it for its proper purpose if space within it was taken up by market stalls and the like. One of the latest Old Testament prophets had foretold how, when representatives of all the nations were to go up to Jerusalem to worship, 'there shall no longer be a trader in the house of the Lord of hosts on that day' (Zech. 14:21). Jesus's prophetic action was designed to enforce this lesson.

But by what authority did he perform such a prophetic action? By what authority did any of the ancient prophets perform prophetic actions? By the authority of God, in whose name they spoke to the people. So, when Jesus was asked, 'Who gave you this authority?' the true answer was 'God'. Why then did he not say so? Because his questioners would not have believed him. He tested them first with another question, to see if they were capable of recognising divine authority when they saw it. Reminding them of John the Baptist's ministry, he asked them whether John's authority was derived 'from heaven (that is, from God) or from men'. This put them on the spot: 'they argued with one another, "If we say, 'From heaven', he will say, 'Why then did you not believe him?' But shall we say, 'From men'?" – they were afraid of the people, for all held that John was a real prophet.' Could they recognise divine authority when it was expressed in the actions and teaching of John? If so, they might be expected to recognise it when it was manifested in the deeds and words of Jesus. But they professed themselves unable to say what the source of John's authority was. So Jesus said to them in effect, 'If you cannot recognise divine authority when you see it in action, no amount of argument will convince you of its presence. If you cannot tell me by what authority John baptised, I will not tell you by what authority I do these things.' There are some people who will demand authority for truth itself, forgetting that truth is the highest authority (see pp. 96–7).

60.

RENDER TO CAESAR

*'Render to Caesar the things that are Caesar's, and to
God the things that are God's'* (Mark 12:17)

For many readers of the Gospels this does not seem to be a
particularly hard saying. They pay their taxes to the state and
give financial support to the Church and various forms of
religious and charitable action, and consider that this is very
much in line with the intention of Jesus's words. There are
others, however, who find in these words material for debate,
arguing that their meaning is not at all clear, or else, if it is clear,
that it is quite different from what it is usually taken to be. Our
first business must be to consider the setting in which the words
were spoken. When we have done that, we may realise that
some of those who heard them felt that here was a hard saying
indeed.

Mark, followed by Matthew (22:15–22) and Luke (20:19–26),
tells how a deputation of Pharisees and Herodians came to
Jesus while he was teaching in the temple precincts during his
last visit to Jerusalem and, expressing their confidence that he
would give them a straight answer, without fear or favour,
asked him if it was lawful to pay taxes to Caesar or not. By
'lawful' they meant 'in accordance with the law of God, the
basis of Israel's corporate life'. Mark says that the questioners
planned 'to entrap him in his talk' (Mark 12:13); Luke spells
this out more explicitly: their purpose, he says, was to 'take
hold of what he said, so as to deliver him up to the authority
and jurisdiction of the governor' (Luke 20:20). The governor or

prefect of Judaea was the representative of Caesar, and any discouragement of the payment of taxes to Caesar would incur sharp retribution from him.

It was, indeed, a very delicate question. After Herod the Great, king of the Jews, died in 4 B.C., the Romans divided his kingdom into three parts, giving each to one of his sons. Galilee, where Jesus lived for most of his life, was ruled by Herod Antipas until A.D. 39. Judaea, the southern part, with Jerusalem as its capital, was given to Archelaus (cf. Matt. 2:22). The sons of Herod received taxes from their subjects, as their father Herod had done. The Herods were not popular, but religiously they were Jews, so no religious difficulties stood in the way of paying taxes to them. But Archelaus's rule in Judaea proved to be so oppressive that, after nine years, the Roman emperor removed him to forestall a revolt, and reorganised Judaea as a Roman province, to be governed by a prefect appointed by himself. From now on the people of Judaea were required to pay their taxes to the Roman emperor, Caesar. A census was held in A.D. 6 to determine the amount of tribute which the new province was to yield.

The Jews had been subject to Gentile overlords for long periods in their history, but no prophet or religious teacher had ever taught in earlier days that there was anything wrong in paying tribute to those overlords. On the contrary, the prophets taught them that if they fell under Gentile domination, this was by God's permission, and they should acknowledge the divine will by paying tribute to their foreign rulers. But around the time of the census in A.D. 6 a new teaching was spread abroad, to the effect that God alone was Israel's king, and therefore it was high treason against him for his people to recognise any Gentile ruler by paying him tribute. The principal teacher of this new doctrine was Judas the Galilean, who led a revolt against the Romans (cf. Acts 5:37). The revolt was crushed, but its ideals lived on, and the propriety of paying taxes to Caesar continued to be a subject for theological debate. It would be generally agreed that Jews in the lands of the Dispersion, living on Gentile territory, should pay taxes in accordance with the laws of the areas where they lived. But the land of Israel was God's land; this was recognised by its inhabitants when they handed over one-tenth of its produce to the maintenance of his temple in Jerusalem. But the taxes which the Roman emperor demanded were also derived from the produce of God's land. Was it right for God's people, living on God's land, to give a proportion of its produce to a pagan ruler? When the question was framed in those terms, the obvious answer for many was 'No'.

What would Jesus say? While he stayed in Galilee the question did not arise: taxes in that region were paid to a Jewish tetrarch. But when he visited Judaea, he came to a place where it was a burning question. However he answered it, it would be almost impossible to avoid giving offence. If he said that it was unlawful to pay taxes to Caesar, the Roman governor would get to hear of it and he could be charged with sedition. If he said that it was lawful, he would offend those who maintained the ideals of Judas the Galilean and many would think him unpatriotic. This would lose him much of his following in Judaea.

'Bring me a denarius,' said Jesus; 'let me see it.' The denarius was a Roman silver coin; Roman taxes had to be paid in Roman coinage. When a denarius was forthcoming, Jesus asked, 'Whose face is this? Whose name is this?' The answer, of course, was 'Caesar's'. Well, said Jesus, the coin which bears Caesar's face and name is obviously Caesar's coin; let Caesar have it back. The verb translated 'render' has the sense of giving back to someone that which belongs to him.

Did he imply that the use of Caesar's coinage was a tacit acknowledgment of Caesar's sovereignty? Perhaps he did. There were some Jews whose orthodoxy was such that they would not look at, let alone handle, a coin which bore a human face. Why? Because it infringed the second commandment of the Decalogue, which forbade the making of 'any likeness of anything that is in heaven above, or that is in the earth beneath, or that is in the water under the earth' (Exod. 20:4). Jesus did not necessarily share this attitude – money of any kind was held in little enough regard by him – but there may have been an implication in his words which the Pharisees among his questioners might have appreciated: such coins were unfit for use by people who were so scrupulous about keeping the law of God, and should go back where they came from. Caesar's coins were best used for paying Caesar's tribute. If that was what Caesar wanted, let him have it; the claims of God were not transgressed by such use of Caesar's money. What was really important was to discover what God's claims were, and see to it that they were met. Once again, he laid primary emphasis on seeking God's kingdom and righteousness.

Some interpreters have discerned more subtle ambiguities in Jesus's answer, as though, for example, he included in 'the things that are God's' the produce of God's land and meant that none of it should go to Caesar, not even when it was converted into Roman coinage. But this kind of interpretation would render the whole business about producing a denarius pointless. Certainly his answer would not satisfy those who believed that for Judaeans to pay tribute to Caesar was wrong. If some of the bystanders had been led by the manner of his entry into Jerusalem a few days before to expect a declaration of independence from him, they must have been disappointed. And indeed, there seems to have been less enthusiasm for him in Jerusalem at the end of Holy Week than there had been at the beginning. On the other hand, if his questioners hoped that he would compromise himself by his reply, they too were disappointed. He not only avoided the dilemma on the horns of which they wished to to impale him, but turned it so as to insist afresh on the central theme of his ministry.

61.

CALL NO MAN YOUR FATHER

'And call no man your father on earth, for you have one Father, who is in heaven' (Matt. 23:9)

In his criticism of the scribes, contained in the discourse of Matthew 23, Jesus speaks disapprovingly of their liking for honorary titles: 'they love ... salutations in the market places, and to be called rabbi by men' (Matt. 23:7). Then he turns to his disciples and tells them not to be like that: 'you are not to be called rabbi, for you have one teacher, and you are all brethren' (Matt. 23:8). 'Rabbi' was a term of respect given by a Jewish disciple to his teacher, and a well-known teacher would be known to the public as Rabbi So-and-so. Jesus was called 'rabbi' by his disciples and by others; it was given to him as a mark of courtesy or respect. For Matthew, however, the word 'rabbi' has a dubious connotation: in his Gospel the only disciple who calls Jesus 'rabbi' is Judas Iscariot, and he does so twice: once at the supper table, when he responds to Jesus's announcement of the presence of a traitor in the company with 'Is it I, rabbi?' (Matt. 26:25), and once in Gethsemane, where the 'Hail, rabbi!' which accompanies his kiss is the sign to the temple police that Jesus is the person to arrest (Matt. 26:49). This attitude to the term 'rabbi' may throw some light on the setting in which Matthew worked and the polemics in which he was engaged.

So, said Jesus to his disciples, refuse all courtesy titles: you have one teacher, and you are all members of one family. Members of a family do not address one another by formal titles, even if some of them indicate high distinction. When John Smith is knighted, his brothers, who have hitherto called him 'John', do not begin to address him to his face as 'Sir John', although others may properly do so. To them he is still 'John'.

But what about calling no man father? Did Jesus mean that his followers ought not to address their fathers in a way that acknowledged their special relationship? It could be thought that he did mean just that, in view of the fact that he is never recorded as calling Mary 'Mother'. But this is unlikely: he is speaking of the use of honorific titles among his disciples. It is equally unlikely that he meant 'Call no man "Abba" but God alone.' For one thing, Matthew's Greek-speaking readers would not naturally take the saying to mean this; for another thing, the whole point of calling God 'Abba' was that this was the ordinary domestic word by which the father was called in the family, and to reserve 'Abba' as a designation for God alone would do away with its significance (see p. 137). But Jesus's meaning could very well have been: In the spiritual sense God alone is your Father; do not give to others the designation which, in that sense, belongs exclusively to him. Jesus was his disciples' teacher, and they called him 'Teacher', but they never called him 'Father'; that was his designation for God.

But did not Paul speak of himself as his converts' father, since, as he said, he had become their 'father in Christ Jesus through the gospel' (1 Cor. 4:15)? He did, but he was using a spiritual analogy, not claiming a title. Well, in insisting on his authority as an 'apostle of Christ Jesus' was he not infringing at least the spirit of Jesus's admonition? No, for again he was not claiming a title but stating a fact: he was indeed commissioned and sent by the risen Lord, and from that was derived the authority with which he spoke. Similarly, if someone is doing the work of a bishop (say) or pastor, then to call him 'Bishop So-and-so' or 'Pastor So-and-so' simply recognises the ministry which he is discharging.

Some Christians, as we know, have interpreted these words of Jesus so literally that they would refrain from the use even of the very democratic 'Mister', perhaps because of its derivation from 'Master', either using no handle at all or preferring something reciprocal like 'Friend' or 'Brother'. Others, considering (probably rightly) that it is the use of honorific titles in religious life that is deprecated by Jesus, would refuse the designation 'The Reverend' to a minister, replacing it by 'Mr.' (which is perfectly proper) or (in writing) putting it between brackets (which is foolish) or even between quotation marks (which is offensive). But, as with so many of Jesus's injunctions, this one can be carried out in a stilted or pettifogging way which destroys the spirit of his teaching. If the local Catholic priest is known throughout the community as Father Jones, I am simply being silly if I persist in calling him something else. If I stop to think what is meant by my calling him Father Jones, I shall probably conclude that he is not *my* father in any sense but that he is no doubt a real father in God to his own congregation. 'Father' in this sense is synonymous with 'Pastor'; the former views the congregation as a family, the latter as a flock of sheep.

When a new bishop arrived in a certain English diocese a few years ago, he quickly let it be known that he did not wish to be addressed as 'my lord'. That, it may be suggested, was a genuine compliance with the spirit of these words of Jesus.

62.

YOU BROOD OF VIPERS

'You serpents, you brood of vipers, how are you to escape being sentenced to hell?' (Matt. 23:33)

The chapter in Matthew's Gospel from which this saying is quoted presents a series of woes pronounced against the scribes and Pharisees – or perhaps we should say laments uttered over them. The series may be regarded as an expansion of Mark 12:38–40, where the people who listened to Jesus as he taught in the temple precincts in Jerusalem during Holy Week were warned against 'the scribes, who like to go about in long robes, and to have salutations in the market places and the best seats in the synagogues and the places of honour at feasts, who devour widows' houses and for a pretence make long prayers. They will receive the greater condemnation.'

The scribes were the recognised exponents of the law. Most of them – certainly most of those who appear in the Gospels – belonged to the party of the Pharisees. The Pharisees traced their spiritual lineage back to the pious groups which, in the days of the Maccabees, resisted all temptations to assimilate their faith and practice to paganising ways, and suffered martyrdom rather than betray their religious heritage. In the first century A.D. they are reckoned to have numbered about 6,000. They banded themselves together in fellowships or brotherhoods, encouraging one another in the defence and practice of the law. The law included not only the written precepts of the Old Testament but the interpretation and application of those precepts – what Mark describes as 'the tradition of the elders' (Mark 7:3). They were greatly concerned about ceremonial purity. This concern forbade them to have social contact with Gentiles, or even with fellow-Jews who were not so particular about the laws of purity as they themselves were. They attached high importance to the tithing of crops (that is, paying ten per cent of the proceeds of harvest into the temple treasury) – not only of grain, wine and olive oil but of garden herbs. They would not willingly eat food, whether in their own houses or in other people's, unless they could be sure that the tithe had been paid on it.

From their viewpoint, they could not help looking on Jesus as dangerously lax, whether in the sovereign freedom with which he disposed of the sabbath law and the food laws or in his readiness to consort with the most questionable persons and actually sit down to a meal with them. It was inevitable that he and they should clash; their conflict, indeed, illustrates the saying about the second-best being the worst enemy of the best.

The Pharisaic way of life lent itself to imitation by people who had no worthier motive than the gaining of a popular reputation for piety. The rabbinical traditions illustrate this fact: seven types of Pharisee are enumerated, and only one of these, the Pharisee who is one for the love of God, receives unqualified commendation.[1] The New Testament picture of the Pharisees is generally an unfavourable one, but more so in the Gospels than in Acts. In Acts they are depicted as not unfriendly to the observant Jewish Christians of Jerusalem: the two groups had this in common (by contrast with the Sadducees), that they believed in the resurrection of the dead.

The gathering together of the woes or laments regarding the Pharisees in Matthew 23 probably reflects the situation in which this Gospel was written, later in the first century, when the Pharisees and the Jewish Christians were engaged in polemical controversy with one another. That provided an opportunity to collect from all quarters criticisms which Jesus had voiced against the Pharisees, and to weave them together into a continuous speech, with its refrain (as commonly translated) 'Woe to you, scribes and Pharisees, hypocrites!'

Pharisees as such were not hypocrites, and Jesus did not say that they were; he was not the one to bear false witness against his neighbour. 'Hypocrite' in New Testament usage means 'play-actor'; it denotes the sort of person who plays a part which is simply assumed for the occasion and does not express his real self. The 'hypocrites' in this repeated denunciation, then, are those who play at being scribes and Pharisees, who 'preach but do not practise' (Matt. 23:3), who assume the actions and words characteristic of scribes and Pharisees without being motivated by true love of God. The genuine Pharisee might disapprove of much that Jesus said and did, but if he was a genuine Pharisee, he was no play-actor. So we might render the recurring refrain of Matthew 23 as 'Alas for you, hypocritical scribes and Pharisees!' – alas for you, because you are incurring a fearful judgment on yourselves.

But what about the 'brood of vipers'? This expression was used by John the Baptist as he saw the crowds coming to listen to his proclamation of judgment and his call to repentance: 'You brood of vipers! Who warned you to flee from the wrath to come?' (Luke 3:7). He compared them to snakes making their way as quickly as possible out of range of an oncoming grass fire. In Matthew 3:7 John directs these words to Pharisees and Sadducees among his hearers. Jesus's use of the same figure may convey a warning that those who pay no heed to impending doom cannot escape it – cannot escape 'the judgment of Gehenna' (to render it literally). And if it is asked how they had incurred this judgment without being aware of it, the answer suggested by Matthew's context would be that by their unreality they were hindering, not helping, others in following the way of righteousness. (In Matthew 12:34 those who charged Jesus with casting out demons by the power of Beelzebul – see p. 89 – are similarly addressed as 'You brood of vipers!')

Finally, Matthew himself apparently indicates that this hard saying, with its context, should be understood as lamentation rather than unmitigated denunciation. For at the end of the discourse, after the statement that the martyr-blood of all generations would be required from that generation (see p. 227),

Matthew places the lament over Jerusalem ('O Jerusalem, Jerusalem ...') which Luke introduces at an earlier point in Jesus's ministry. It is easy to see why Luke introduces it where he does: Jesus has been warned in Galilee that Herod Antipas wants to kill him, and he replies that that cannot be, since Jerusalem is the proper place for a prophet to be put to death (Luke 13:31–33). Then comes 'O Jerusalem, Jerusalem, killing the prophets ...' (verses 34–35). Actually, the lament would be *chronologically* appropriate if it were uttered at the end of Jesus's last visit to Jerusalem before the final one, for it ends with the words: 'You will not see me until you say, "Blessed is he who comes in the name of the Lord"' (Luke 13:35; Matt. 23:39). This may simply mean, 'You will not see me until festival time'. (T. W. Manson compares two people parting today and saying, 'Next time we meet we shall be singing "O come, all ye faithful"', i.e. 'Next time we meet will be Christmas'[2].) But Luke and Matthew place the lament in contexts where it is *topically* appropriate; Matthew in particular, by placing it where he does (Matt. 23:37–39), communicates something of the sorrow with which Jesus found it necessary to speak as he did about those who should have been trustworthy guides but in fact were leading their followers to disaster.

63.

THIS GENERATION WILL NOT
PASS AWAY

*'Truly, I say to you, this generation will not pass away
before all these things take place'* (Mark 13:30)

This has been regarded as a hard saying by those who take it to
refer to Christ's second advent, his coming in glory. If Jesus
really affirmed that this event would take place within a
generation from the time of speaking (which was only a few
days before his arrest and execution), then, it is felt, he was
mistaken, and this is for many an unacceptable conclusion.

Although this saying is not one of P. W. Schmiedel's pillar
passages, many have defended its genuineness on the ground
that no one would have invented an unfulfilled prophecy and
put it on Jesus's lips. If an unfulfilled prophecy is ascribed to
him in the gospel tradition, that can only be (they have argued)
because he actually uttered it. In more recent times, however,
the utterance has been widely ascribed not to the historical
Jesus but to some prophet in the early Church speaking in
Jesus's name. Rudolf Bultmann regarded the discourse of
Mark 13:5-27 as 'a Jewish apocalypse with a Christian editing',
and thought that this utterance would have made a suitable
conclusion to such an apocalypse.[1]

Some students of the New Testament who do not concede
that Jesus might have been mistaken are nevertheless
convinced that the reference is indeed to his glorious advent. If
'all these things' must denote the events leading up to the
advent and the advent itself, then some other interpretation,

they say, will have to be placed on 'this generation'. Other meanings which the Greek noun *genea* (here translated 'generation') bears in certain contexts are canvassed. The word is sometimes used in the sense of 'race', so perhaps, it is suggested, the point is that the Jewish race, or even the human race, will not pass away before the second advent. Plainly the idea that the human race is meant cannot be entertained; every description of that event implies that human beings will be around to witness it, for otherwise it would have no context to give it any significance. Nor is there much more to be said for the idea that the Jewish race is meant: there is no hint anywhere in the New Testament that the Jewish race will cease to exist before the end of the world. In any case, what point would there be in such a vague prediction? It would be as much as to say, 'At some time in the indefinite future all these things will take place.'

'This generation' is a recurring phrase in the Bible, and each time it is used it bears the ordinary sense of the people belonging, as we say, to one fairly comprehensive age-group. One desperate attempt to combine the recognition of this fact with a reference to the second advent in the text we are considering, and yet exonerate Jesus from being mistaken in his forecast, is to take 'this generation' to mean not 'this generation now alive' but 'the generation which will be alive at the time about which I am speaking'. The meaning would then be: 'The generation on earth when these things begin to take place will still be on earth when they are all completed: all these things will take place within the span of one generation.'[2]

Is this at all probable? I think not. When we are faced with the problem of understanding a hard saying, it is always a safe procedure to ask, 'What would it have meant to the people who first heard it?' And there can be but one answer to this question in relation to the present hard saying. Jesus's hearers could have understood him to mean only that 'all these things' would take place within *their* generation. Not only does 'generation' in the phrase 'this generation' always mean the people alive at one particular time; the phrase itself always means 'the generation now living'. Jesus spoke of 'this generation' in this sense several times, and generally in no flattering terms. In fact, his use of the phrase echoes its use in the Old Testament records of the Israelites' wilderness wanderings. The generation of Israelites that left Egypt did not survive to enter Canaan; it died out in the wilderness – all the adults, that is to say (with two named exceptions). And why? Because it refused to accept the word of God communicated through Moses. Hence it is called 'this evil generation' (Deut. 1:35), 'a perverse and crooked generation' (Deut. 32:5).

Similarly the generation to which Jesus ministered is called 'an evil generation' (Luke 11:29), 'this adulterous and sinful generation' (Mark 8:38), because of its unbelief and unresponsiveness. 'The men of Nineveh', said Jesus, 'will arise at the judgment with this generation and condemn it; for they repented at the preaching of Jonah, and behold, something greater than Jonah is here' (Luke 11:32; see p. 97). In fact, 'this generation' has so capped the unhappy record of its predecessors that all their misdeeds will be visited on it: 'Yes, I tell you, it shall be required of this generation' (Luke 11:51). The phrase 'this generation' is found too often on Jesus's lips in this literal sense for us to suppose that it suddenly takes on a different meaning in the saying which we are now examining. Moreover, if the generation of the end-time had been intended, '*that* generation' would have been a more natural way of referring to it than 'this generation'.

But what are 'all these things' which are due to take place before 'this generation' passes away? Jesus was speaking in response to a question put to him by four of his disciples. They were visiting Jerusalem for the Passover, and the disciples were impressed by the architectural grandeur of the temple, so recently restored and enlarged by Herod. 'Look, Teacher,' said one of them, 'what wonderful stones and what wonderful buildings!' Jesus replied, 'Do you see these great buildings? There will not be left here one stone upon another, that will not be thrown down.' This aroused their curiosity and, seizing an opportunity when they were with him on the Mount of Olives, looking across to the temple area, four of them asked, 'Tell us, when will this be? And what will be the sign when all these things are to be accomplished?' (Mark 13:1–4).

In the disciples' question, 'all these things' are the destruction of the temple and attendant events. It seems reasonable to regard the hard saying as summing up the answer to their question. If so, then 'all these things' will have the same meaning in question and answer. The hard saying will then mean, 'this generation will not pass away before' the temple is totally destroyed. It is well known that the temple was actually destroyed by the Romans under the crown prince Titus in August of A.D. 70, not more than forty years after Jesus spoke. Forty years is not too long a period to be called a generation; in fact, forty years is the conventional length of a generation in the biblical vocabulary. It was certainly so with the 'evil generation' of the wilderness wanderings: 'Forty years long was I grieved with this generation', said God (Ps. 95:10, Prayer Book version).

But if that is what the saying means, why should it have been thought to predict the last advent within that generation? Because, in the discourse which intervenes between verse 4 and verse 30 of Mark 13, other subject-matter is interwoven with the forecast of the time of trouble leading up to the disaster of A.D. 70. In particular, there is the prediction of 'the Son of man coming in clouds with power and great glory' (see p. 246) and sending out his angels to 'gather his elect from the four winds, from the ends of the earth to the ends of heaven' (verses 26–27). Some interpreters have taken this to be a highly figurative description of the divine judgment which many Christians, and not only Christians, saw enacted in the Roman siege and destruction of Jerusalem; but it is difficult to agree with them.

Mark probably wrote his Gospel four or five years before A.D. 70. When he wrote, the fall of the temple and the coming of the Son of man lay alike in the future, and he had no means of knowing whether or not there would be a substantial lapse of time between these two events. Even so, he preserves in the same context another saying of Jesus relating to the time of a future event: 'But of that day or that hour no one knows, not even the angels in heaven, nor the Son, but only the Father' (Mark 13:32). This saying was listed by Schmiedel among his pillar texts, on the ground that a saying in which Jesus admits his ignorance (even if only in one respect) would not have been invented or ascribed to him by the early Church. But what is the day or hour to which it refers? Certainly not the day or hour of the destruction of the temple: what the whole context, and not only the hard saying of verse 30, emphasises about that event is its nearness and certainty. The event whose timing is known to none but the Father cannot be anything other than the coming of the Son of man, described in verse 26.

Luke, as he reproduces the substance of the discourse of Mark 13:5-30, lays more emphasis on the fate of Jerusalem, the city as well as the temple: 'Jerusalem will be trodden down by the Gentiles, until the times of the Gentiles are fulfilled' (Luke 21:24). When 'the times of the Gentiles' (the period of Gentile domination of the holy city) will be fulfilled is not indicated. But this saying, though peculiar to Luke in the gospel record, is not Luke's invention: it turns up again in the Apocalypse, and in a part of it which is probably earlier than that work as a whole and was subsequently incorporated into it. The outer court of the temple, John is told, 'is given over to the nations (Gentiles), and they will trample over the holy city for forty-two months' (Rev. 11:2). This is a prophetic utterance communicated to John by a voice from heaven, but it has the same origin as the words recorded in Luke 21:24.

Matthew, writing his Gospel probably a short time after the destruction of the temple, could see, as Mark naturally could not, the separation in time between that event and the coming of the Son of man. For Matthew, the one event had taken place, while the other was still future. He rewords the disciples' question to Jesus so that it refers to both events distinctly and explicitly. Jesus, as in Mark, foretells how not one stone of the temple will be left standing on another, and the disciples say, 'Tell us, (a) when will these things be, and (b) what will be the sign of your coming and of the close of the age?' (Matt. 24:3). Then, at the end of the following discourse, Jesus answers their twofold question by saying that (a) 'this generation will not pass away till all *these things* take place' (Matt. 24:34) while, (b) with regard to his coming and 'the close of the age', he tells them that 'of *that* day and hour no one knows, not even the angels of heaven, nor the Son, but the Father only' (Matt. 24:36). The distinction between the two predictions is clear in Matthew, for whom the earlier of the two predicted events now lay in the past; but it was already implicit, though not so clear, in Mark.

64.

THERE THE EAGLES WILL BE
GATHERED TOGETHER

*'Wherever the body is, there the eagles will be gathered
together'* (Matt. 24:28; Luke 17:37)

There is a slight difference between the two forms of this saying
which does not appear in the English of the RSV (quoted
above): in Matthew the Greek word translated 'body' means
specifically a dead body, whereas Luke uses the more general
word for 'body', alive or dead, although in the present context a
dead body is implied.

The saying gives the impression of being a proverbial
utterance, applied (as proverbial utterances regularly are) to
some appropriate situation. But are the birds of prey
mentioned in the saying really eagles? Might we not have
expected a reference to vultures? Yes indeed; but there are two
points to be made.

First, the Hebrew word normally translated 'eagle' in the Old
Testament appears occasionally to denote the vulture. 'Make
yourselves as bald as the eagle', the people of Judah are told in
Mic. 1:16; but it is the vulture, not the eagle, that is bald. In
those places where the Hebrew word for 'eagle' seems to have the
meaning 'vulture', it is the Greek word for 'eagle' that is used in
the Greek version of the Old Testament; so that for Matthew
and Luke there was this precedent for the occasional use of the
Greek word for 'eagle' in the sense of 'vulture'.

Next, even if (as is probable) the proverbial utterance
referred originally to vultures, the change to 'eagles' may have

been made deliberately, if not in the Aramaic that Jesus spoke, then in the Greek version of his words on which the Gospels of Matthew and Luke drew. 'Where there is a dead body the vultures will flock together' means in effect, 'Where there is a situation ripe for judgment, there the judgment will fall.' But the situation in view in the context is the city of Jerusalem, doomed to destruction because of its unwillingness to pay heed to the message of peace which Jesus brought. The executioners of this particular judgment were Roman legionary forces. The eagle was the standard of a Roman legion, and this may explain the choice of the word 'eagles' here.

T. W. Manson, who prefers the rendering 'vultures' here and sees no reference to the Roman military eagles, thinks the point of the saying is the swiftness with which vultures discover the presence of carrion and flock to feast on it.[1] So swiftly will the judgment fall 'on the day when the Son of man is revealed' (Luke 17:30).

In Luke's account, but not in Matthew's, the saying is Jesus's reply to a question asked by the disciples. He has just told them how, on that day, the judgment will seize on one person and pass over another, separating two people asleep in the same bed or two women grinding at one mill (one of them turning the upper stone and the other pouring in the grain). 'Where, Lord?' say the disciples – possibly meaning, 'Where will this judgment take place?' To this his answer is, 'Wherever there is a situation which calls for it.'

Among several instances of the kind of proverbial utterance illustrated by this saying special mention may be made of Job 39:27–30:

> Is it at your command that the eagle mounts up
>   and makes his nest on high?
> On the rock he dwells and makes his home
>   in the fastness of the rocky crag.
> Thence he spies out the prey;
>   his eyes behold it afar off.
> His young ones suck up blood;
>   and where the slain are, there is he.

65.

I DO NOT KNOW YOU

'Afterward the other maidens came also, saying, "Lord, lord, open to us." But he replied, "Truly, I say to you, I do not know you"' (Matt. 25:11-12)

The picture of people arriving after the door has been shut and finding it impossible to gain entrance appears elsewhere in the teaching of Jesus. In Luke 13:25-28 Jesus speaks of such people who, seeing themselves shut out, protest to the master of the house, 'We ate and drank in your presence, and you taught in our streets.' But even so they are refused admittance; they are excluded from the kingdom of God. Matthew's version of the Sermon on the Mount contains a parallel to that passage in Luke; in Matthew's account those who are shut out produce what might be regarded as even stronger credentials entitling them to admittance: 'did we not prophesy in your name, and cast out demons in your name, and do many mighty works in your name?' (Matt. 7:22) – but all to no avail.

The most memorable setting of the picture, however, is in the parable of the ten virgins, as it is traditionally called. The haunting pathos of the late-comers finding the door closed in their faces was caught and expressed by Tennyson in the song, 'Late, late, so late! and dark the night and chill!' which was sung to Guinevere by the little maid in the nunnery where the queen had sought sanctuary. True, in the scene from real life depicted in the parable the maidens' disappointment was keen, but they suffered no irreparable loss: they had missed the wedding feast, indeed, but there would be other wedding feasts, and they would remember to take an adequate supply of oil another time. But in the application of the parable the loss is more serious.

The parable is one of three which Matthew appends to his version of Jesus's Olivet discourse – the discourse which has its climax in the glorious coming of the Son of man.

There was a wedding in the village. A wedding story with no mention of the bride seems very odd to us, but different times and different lands have different customs. Just possibly she does receive a mention, but if so, only in passing: some authorities for the text of Matthew 25:1 say that the ten maidens 'went to meet the bridegroom *and the bride*'. The ten maidens do not appear to have been bridesmaids, or even specially invited guests; they were girls of the village who had decided to form a torchlight procession and escort the bridegroom and his party to the house where the wedding feast was to be held. They knew that, if they did so, there would be a place at the feast for them, so that they could share in the good cheer. To this day there are parts of the world where a wedding feast is a public occasion for the neighbourhood, and all who come find a welcome and something to eat and drink.

No time was announced for the bridegroom to set out for the feast, and the day wore on. That was all right: a torchlight procession is more impressive in the dark. The 'torches' were long poles with oil-lamps tied to the top, and the more provident girls took a supply of olive oil with them in case the lamps went out. As the evening wore on and the bridegroom still did not come, one after another dropped off to sleep. However, their lamps were lit, ready for the warning shout. Suddenly the shout came: 'Here he is!' They set off to join his party, but as they trimmed the wicks of their lamps, five of them found that their lamps were going out, and they had no extra oil. The others could not lend them any of theirs, for then there would not be enough to last the journey. So the improvident girls had to go and buy some, and that would not be too easy at midnight; yet by persistence they managed at last to get some. But by that time they were too late to join the procession, and when they reached the house, they could not get in. They hammered on the street-door and shouted to the door-keeper, 'O sir! O sir! please let us in.' But all the answer they received was 'No; I don't know you.' So they had to go back home in the dark, tired and disappointed, because they had not been ready.

The oil was good oil, while it lasted; but the oil that was used yesterday will not keep today's lamps alight. So perhaps we may learn not to depend exclusively on past experiences; they will not be sufficient for the needs of the present. Daily grace must be obtained for daily need. The explicit lesson attached to the parable is: 'Keep awake, for you know neither the day nor the hour' (Matt. 25:13). Later forms of the text (represented by the AV) add the words: 'when the Son of man comes'. Certainly in the context of the parable those words are implied, but the fact that the evangelist did not include them suggests that the parable has a more general application. Keep awake, because a time of testing may come without warning. Be ready to resist this temptation (whatever form it may take); be ready to meet this crisis; be ready to grasp this opportunity. Somebody needs help; be ready to give it, 'for you know neither the day nor the hour' when the call may come.

66.

THIS IS MY BODY ... THIS IS MY BLOOD

> *And as they were eating, he took bread, and blessed, and broke it, and gave it to them, and said, 'Take; this is my body.' And he took a cup, and when he had given thanks he gave it to them, and they all drank of it. And he said to them, 'This is my blood of the covenant, which is poured out for many'* (Mark 14:22–24)

The words of institution, spoken by Jesus at the Last Supper, were not intended by him to be hard sayings; but they may be included among his hard sayings if regard is had to the disputes and divisions to which their interpretation has given rise.

Mark's version of the words, quoted above, is not the earliest record of them in the New Testament. Paul reproduces them in 1 Corinthians 11:23–25, written in A.D. 55. He reminds his converts in Corinth that he 'delivered' this record to them by word of mouth (presumably when he came to their city to preach the gospel in A.D. 50), and says that he himself 'received' it 'from the Lord' even earlier (presumably soon after his conversion); he had received it, that is to say, through a (no doubt short) chain of transmission which went back to Jesus himself and derived its authority from him. There are differences in wording between Paul's version and Mark's, perhaps reflecting variations in usage among the churches of the first Christian generation, but we are not concerned here with those differences; it is more important to consider the meaning of what the two versions have in common.

The Last Supper was most probably a Passover meal. It may

be that Jesus and his disciples kept the Passover (on this occasion, if not on others) a day earlier than the official date of the feast fixed by the temple authorities in Jerusalem. At the Passover meal, which commemorated the deliverance of the Israelites from Egypt many centuries before, there was unleavened bread and red wine on the table, as well as food of other kinds. In the explanatory narrative which preceded the meal, the bread was said to be 'the bread of affliction which our fathers ate when they left Egypt' (cf. Deut. 16:3). A literal-minded person might say that the bread on the table was not the bread which the exodus generation ate: that bread was no longer available. But to the faith of the eaters it *was* the same bread: they were encouraged to identify themselves with the exodus generation, for 'in each generation', the prescription ran, 'it is a duty to regard oneself as though one had oneself been brought up out of Egypt'.

At the outset of the meal the head of the family, having broken bread, gave thanks for it in time-honoured language: 'Blessed art thou, O Lord our God, King of the universe, who bringest forth bread from the earth.' But at the Last Supper Jesus, as head of his 'family', having given thanks for the bread, added words which gave the bread a new significance: 'Take it,' he said to the disciples, 'this is my body.' The Pauline version continues, '... my body which is for you; do this as my memorial'. The Passover meal was a memorial of the great deliverance at the time of the exodus; now a new memorial was being instituted in view of a new and greater deliverance about to be accomplished. And if any literal-minded person were to say, 'But the bread which he took from the table could not be his body; the disciples could see his living body there before their eyes,' once again the answer would be that it is to the faith of the eaters that the bread is the Lord's body; it is by faith that, in the eating of the memorial bread, they participate in his life.

At the end of the meal, when the closing blessing or 'grace after meat' had been said, a cup of wine was shared by the family. This cup, called the 'cup of blessing', was the third of four cups which stood on the table. When Jesus had said the blessing and given this cup to his companions, without drinking from it himself, he said to them, 'This is my covenant blood, which is poured out for many.' (The Pauline version says, 'This is the new covenant in my blood, which is poured out for you; do this as my memorial, every time you drink it.')

When Moses, at the foot of Mount Sinai, read the law of God to the Israelites who had come out of Egypt and they had undertaken to keep it, the blood of sacrificed animals was sprinkled partly on the altar (representing the presence of God) and partly on the people, and Moses spoke of it as 'the blood of the covenant which the Lord has made with you in accordance with all these words' (Exod. 24:3-8). To the disciples, who had the passover and exodus narratives vividly in their minds at that time, Jesus's words must have meant that a new covenant was about to be instituted in place of that into which their ancestors were brought in Moses' day - to be instituted, moreover, by Jesus's death for his people. If, then, when they take the memorial bread they participate by faith in the life of him who died and rose again, so when they take the cup they declare and appropriate by faith their 'interest in the Saviour's blood'. In doing so, they enter by experience into the meaning of his words of institution and know that through him they are members of God's covenant community.

Matthew (26:26-29) reproduces Mark's version of the words, his main amplification of them being the explanatory phrase 'for the forgiveness of sins' after 'poured out for many'. In Luke 22:17-20 we find (according to the information in the margin or footnotes) both a longer and a shorter version; the longer version has close affinities with Paul's. On John 6:53-55 see pp. 21-5.

Luke's account is specially important because he is the only evangelist who reports Jesus as saying, 'Do this in remembrance of me' (Luke 22:19). In his account these words are added to those spoken over the bread (in Paul's account they are attached both to the bread and to the cup). From Mark's account (and Matthew's) it might not have been gathered that this was anything other than a once-for-all eating and drinking; Luke makes it plain that the eating and drinking were meant to be repeated.

According to all three synoptic evangelists Jesus said, while giving his disciples the cup, 'I shall not drink again of the fruit of the vine until that day when I drink it new in the kingdom of God' – or words to the same effect (Mark 14:25; cf. Matt. 26:29; Luke 22:18). He would fast until the kingdom of God was established; then the heavenly banquet would begin. But when he rose from the dead, he made himself known to his disciples 'in the breaking of the bread' (Luke 24:35); Peter in the house of Cornelius tells how he and his companions 'ate and drank with him after he rose from the dead' (Acts 10:41). This suggests that the kingdom of which he spoke at the Last Supper has now come in some sense (it has 'come with power', in the language of Mark 9:1): it has been inaugurated, even if its consummation lies in the future. Until that consummation his people continue to 'do this' – to take the bread and wine – as his memorial, and as they do so, they consciously realise his presence with them.

67

LET HIM WHO HAS NO SWORD BUY ONE

'But now, let him ... who has no sword sell his mantle and buy one' (Luke 22:36)

This is a hard saying in the sense that it is difficult to reconcile it with Jesus's general teaching on violence: violence was not the course for his followers to take. It is widely held that this saying was not meant to be taken literally, but if so, how was it meant to be taken?

It occurs in Luke's Gospel only. Luke reports it as part of a conversation between Jesus and his disciples at the Last Supper. Jesus reminds them of an earlier occasion when he sent them out on a missionary tour and told them to take neither purse (for money) nor bag (for provisions) nor sandals. Presumably, they could expect their needs to be supplied by well-disposed people along their route (Luke 10:4-7). But now things were going to be different: people would be reluctant to show them hospitality, for they might get into trouble for doing so. On that earlier occasion, as the disciples now agreed, they had lacked nothing. 'But now,' said Jesus, 'let him who has a purse take it, and likewise a bag' – they would have to fend for themselves. More than that: 'let him who has no sword sell his cloak and buy one'. If that is surprising, more surprising still is the reason he gives for this change of policy: 'For I tell you that this scripture must be fulfilled in me, "And he was reckoned with transgressors", for what is written about me has its fulfilment.'

It is doubtful if the disciples followed his reasoning here, but they thought they had got the point about the sword. No need to worry about that: 'Look, Lord,' they said, 'here are two swords.' To which he replied, 'It is enough' or, perhaps, 'Enough of this.'

Luke certainly does not intend his readers to understand the words literally. He goes on to tell how, a few hours later, when Jesus was arrested, one of the disciples let fly with a sword – probably one of the two which they had produced at the supper table – and cut off an ear of the high priest's slave. But Jesus said, 'No more of this!' and healed the man's ear with a touch (Luke 22:49–51).

So what did he mean by his reference to selling one's cloak to buy a sword? He himself was about to be condemned as a criminal, 'reckoned with transgressors', to use language applied to the Servant of the Lord in Isaiah 53:12. Those who until now had been his associates would find themselves treated as outlaws; they could no longer count on the charity of sympathetic fellow-Israelites. Purse and bag would now be necessary. Josephus tells us that when Essenes went on a journey they had no need to take supplies with them, for they knew that their needs would be met by fellow-members of their order; they did, however, carry arms to protect themselves against bandits.[1]

But Jesus does not envisage bandits as the kind of people against whom his disciples would require protection: they themselves would be lumped together with bandits by the authorities, and they might as well act the part properly and carry arms, as bandits did. Taking him literally, they revealed that they had anticipated his advice: they already had two swords. This incidentally shows how far they were from resembling a band of Zealot insurgents: such a band would have been much more adequately equipped. And the words with which Jesus concluded the conversation did not mean that two swords would be enough; they would have been ludicrously insufficient against the band that came to arrest him, armed with swords and clubs. He meant 'Enough of this!' – they had misunderstood his sad irony, and it was time to drop the subject. T. W. Manson rendered the words 'Well, well'. In contrast to the days when they had shared their Master's popularity, 'they are now surrounded by enemies so ruthless that the possession of two swords will not help the situation.'[2]

This text ... has nothing to say directly on the question whether armed resistance to injustice and evil is ever justifiable. It is simply a vivid pictorial way of describing the complete change which has come about in the temper and attitude of the Jewish people since the days of the disciples' mission. The disciples understood the saying literally and so missed the point; but that is no reason why we should follow their example.[3]

68.

WHY ARE YOU HERE?

Jesus said to him, 'Friend, why are you here?' (Matt. 26:50)

These are the words spoken by Jesus to Judas on receiving the traitor's kiss from him in Gethsemane, as rendered in the RSV text. Almost certainly they are a mistranslation. The alternative rendering given in the margin or footnote is better: 'do that for which you have come'. Similarly the NEB text gives the rendering: 'Friend, do what you are here to do'; the NIV text says, 'Friend, do what you came for.'

The Greek word translated 'friend' is used by Matthew alone of the New Testament writers; it might be translated 'companion', 'comrade' or 'mate'. Judas is the only person whom Jesus addresses thus. The same vocative is used in two parables: by the owner of the vineyard to the workman who protested at the lavishness with which the last-hired men were paid ·(Matt. 20:13; see p. 197) and by the king who gave a marriage feast for his son to the man who came without a wedding garment (Matt. 22:12; see p. 206). On Jesus's lips it was particularly appropriate as a term of address to a man who, an hour or two before, had sat at table with him and 'dipped his hand in the dish' with him (Matt. 26:23).

The rest of the sentence might be translated literally 'that for which you are here'. It seems to be an adjectival clause; the principal clause would then be an imperative like 'Do'. The clause has turned up as an inscription on a few goblets of the New Testament period, suitable for use at drinking parties, where the principal verb supplied is 'Be of good cheer' or 'Enjoy yourself'.[1] The complete inscription means 'Enjoy yourself; that's what you're here for.' Matthew uses the clause in a much more solemn, and indeed tragic, setting; but his meaning is illuminated by the inscription. Jesus says in effect to Judas, 'You know what you are here for; get on with it!'

One further suggestion is that the clause might be an exclamation, as though Jesus said, 'Friend, what a thing you are here for!' But it is best to take it as an adjectival clause, and to render the words, 'Friend, do what you have come to do.'

69.

YOU WILL SEE THE SON OF MAN

Again the high priest asked him, 'Are you the Christ, the Son of the Blessed?' And Jesus said, 'I am; and you will see the Son of man sitting at the right hand of Power, and coming with the clouds of heaven' (Mark 14:61–62; cf. Matt. 26:63–64; Luke 22:67–70)

After his arrest in Gethsemane, Jesus was brought before a court of enquiry, presided over by the high priest. At first, according to Mark's narrative, an attempt was made to convict him of having spoken against the Jerusalem temple. Not only was violation of the sanctity of the temple, whether in deed or in word, a capital offence; it was the one type of offence for which the Roman government allowed the supreme Jewish court to pass and execute sentence at its own discretion. Two or three years later, when Stephen was successfully prosecuted before the supreme court on a similar charge, there was no need to refer the case to Pilate before execution could be carried out. On the present occasion, however, Jesus could not be convicted on this charge because the two witnesses for the prosecution gave conflicting evidence.

Then the high priest, apparently on his own initiative, asked Jesus to tell the court if he was the Messiah, the Son of God. (He used 'the Blessed' as a substitute for the divine name.) The Messiah was entitled to be described as the Son of God, if he was the person addressed by God in Psalm 2:7 with the words, 'You are my son', or the person who in Psalm 89:26 cries to God, 'Thou art my Father'. Jesus was not in the way of spontaneously referring to himself as the Messiah. But to the high priest's question he answered 'I am.' How Matthew and Luke understood this reply may be seen from their renderings of it: 'You have said so' (Matt. 26:64) or 'You say that I am' (Luke 22:70). That is to say, if Jesus must give an answer to the high priest's question, the answer cannot be other than 'Yes', but the choice of words is the high priest's, not his own. The words that followed, however, were his own choice. It is as though he said, 'If "Christ" (that is, "Messiah" or "Anointed One") is the term you insist on using, then I have no option but to say "Yes", but if I were to choose my own terms, I should say that you will see the Son of man sitting at the right hand of the Almighty and coming with the clouds of heaven.' (Here 'Power' on Jesus's lips, meaning much the same as we mean when we say 'the Almighty', is, like 'the Blessed' on the high priest's lips, a substitute for the divine name.)

What, then, does this saying mean, and why was it declared blasphemous by the high priest? It means, in brief, that while the Son of man, Jesus himself, stood now before his judges friendless and humiliated, they would one day see him vindicated by God. He says this in symbolic language, but the source of this symbolic language is biblical. Mention has been made already of the Son of man coming with the clouds of heaven (see p. 228); this language is drawn from Daniel 7:13-14, where 'one like a son of man' is seen in a vision coming 'with the clouds of heaven' to be presented before God ('the Ancient of Days') and to receive eternal world dominion from him. The 'one like a son of man' is a human figure, displacing the succession of beast-like figures who had been exercising world dominion previously. The one whose claims received such scant courtesy from his judges would yet be acknowledged as sovereign lord in the hearts of men and women throughout the world. His claims would, moreover, be acknowledged by God: the Son of man would be seen seated 'at the right hand of the Almighty'. This wording is taken from Psalm 110:1, which records a divine oracle addressed certainly to the ruler of David's line: 'Sit at my right hand, till I make your enemies your footstool.' The present prisoner at the bar would be seen to be, by divine appointment, lord of the universe – and that not in the distant future, but forthwith. '*From now on*', in Luke's version, 'the Son of man shall be seated at the right hand of the power of God' (Luke 22:69; see p. 154). (Luke omits the language about the clouds of heaven.) '*Henceforth*', in Matthew's version, 'you will see the Son of man seated at the right hand of Power, and coming on the clouds of heaven.' The right hand of God was the place of supreme exaltation; the clouds were the vehicle of the divine glory.

The Servant of the Lord in the Old Testament, once despised and rejected by men, was hailed by God as 'exalted, extolled and made very high' (Isa. 52:13–53:3); this role is filled in the New Testament by Jesus, obedient to the point of death, and death by crucifixion at that, being thereupon 'highly exalted' by God and endowed with 'the name which is above every name', in order to be confessed by every tongue as Lord (Phil. 2:6–11). It is the same reversal of roles that is announced in Jesus's reply to the high priest.

Why was his reply judged to be blasphemous? Not because he agreed that he was the Messiah: that might be politically dangerous and could be interpreted as seditious by the Roman administration (as indeed it was), but it did not encroach on the prerogatives of God; neither did the claim to be Son of God in *that* sense. But the language which he went on to use by his own choice did appear to be an invasion of the glory that belongs to God alone. It was there that blasphemy was believed to lie. The historical sequel may be allowed to rule on the question whether it was blasphemy or an expression of faith in God which was justified in the event.

70

WHY HAST THOU FORSAKEN ME?

And at the ninth hour Jesus cried with a loud voice, 'Eloi, Eloi, lama sabachthani?' which means, 'My God, my God, why hast thou forsaken me?' (Mark 15:34; cf. Matt. 27:46)

This is the hardest of all the hard sayings. It is the last articulate utterance of the crucified Jesus reported by Mark and Matthew; soon afterwards, they say, with a loud cry (the content of which is not specified) he breathed his last.

P. W. Schmiedel adduced this utterance as one of the few 'absolutely credible' texts which might be used as 'foundation-pillars for a truly scientific life of Jesus', on the ground that it could not be a product of the worship of Jesus in the Church. No one would have invented it; it was an uncompromising datum of tradition which an evangelist had either to reproduce as it stood or else pass over without mention.

It would be wise not to make the utterance a basis for reconstructing the inner feelings which Jesus experienced on the cross. The question 'Why?' was asked, but remained unanswered. There are some theologians and psychologists, nevertheless, who have undertaken to supply the answer which the record does not give: their example is not to be followed. This at least must be said: if it is a hard saying for the reader of the Gospels, it was hardest of all for our Lord himself. The assurances on which men and women of God in Old Testament times rested in faith were not for him. 'Many are the afflictions of the righteous, but the Lord delivers him out of them all', said a psalmist (Ps. 34:19), but for Jesus no deliverance appeared.

It seems certain that the words are quoted from the beginning of Psalm 22. Arguments to the contrary are not convincing. The words are not quoted from the Hebrew text, but from an Aramaic paraphrase. (For the Aramaic form *Eloi*, 'my God', in Mark, the Hebrew form *Eli* appears in Matthew. Any attempt to determine the precise pronunciation would have to reckon with the fact that some bystanders thought that Jesus was calling for Elijah to come and help him.) Psalm 22, while it begins with a cry of utter desolation, is really an expression of faith and thanksgiving; the help from God, so long awaited and even despaired of, comes at last. So it has sometimes been thought that, while Jesus is recorded as uttering only the opening cry of desolation, in fact he recited the whole psalm (although inaudibly) as an expression of faith.

This cannot be proved, but there is one New Testament writer who seems to have thought so – the author of the letter to the Hebrews. This writer more than once quotes other passages from Psalm 22 apart from the opening cry and ascribes them to Jesus. In particular, he says that Jesus 'offered up prayers and supplications, with loud crying and tears, to him who was able to save him from death, and he was heard for his godly fear; Son though he was, he learned obedience through what he suffered, and being made perfect he became the source of eternal salvation to all who obey him' (Heb. 5:7-9).

In these words the writer to the Hebrews expounds, in terms of the sufferings which Jesus endured, the acknowledgment of Psalm 22:24: God 'has not despised or abhorred the affliction of the afflicted; and he has not hid his face from him, but has heard, when he cried to him'. But when he says that Jesus's prayer 'to him who was able to save him from death' was answered, he does not mean that Jesus was delivered from dying; he means that, having died, he was 'brought again from the dead' to live henceforth 'by the power of an indestructible life' (Heb. 13:20; 7:16).

The same writer presents Jesus in his death as being a willing and acceptable sacrifice to God. That martyrs in Israel should offer their lives to expiate the sins of others was not unprecedented. Instead of having his heart filled with bitter resentment against those who were treating him so abominably, Jesus in dying offered his life to God as an atonement for their sins, and for the sins of the world. Had he not said on one occasion that 'the Son of man came ... to give his life a ransom for many' (Mark 10:45)? But now he did so the more effectively by entering really into the desolation of that God-forsakenness which is the lot of sinners – by being 'made sin for us', as Paul puts it (2 Cor. 5:21). 'In His death everything was made His that sin had made ours – everything in sin except its sinfulness.'[1]

Jesus 'learned obedience through what he suffered', as the writer to the Hebrews says, in the sense that by his suffering he learned the cost of his wholehearted obedience to his Father. His acceptance of the cross crowned his obedience, and he was never more pleasing to the Father than in this act of total devotion; yet that does not diminish the reality of his experience of being God-forsaken. But this reality has made him the more effective as the deliverer and supporter of his people. He is no visitant from another world, avoiding too much involvement with this world of ours; he has totally involved himself in the human lot. There is no depth of dereliction known to human beings which he has not plumbed; by this means he has been 'made perfect' – that is to say, completely qualified to be his people's sympathising helper in their most extreme need. If they feel like crying to God, 'Why hast thou forsaken me?', they can reflect that that is what he cried. When they call out of the depths to God, he who called out of the depths on Good Friday knows what it feels like. But there is this difference: he is with them now to strengthen them – no one was there to strengthen him.

NOTES TO TEXT

Introduction

1. The material common to Matthew and Luke but not found in Mark is conventionally labelled Q. The teaching peculiar to Matthew is labelled M; that peculiar to Luke is labelled L.
2. T.W. Manson, *The Teaching of Jesus*, second edition (Cambridge, 1935).
3. T.W. Manson, *The Sayings of Jesus*, second edition (London, 1949).
4. *The Sayings*, p. 35.

Chapter 1

1. Augustine, *On Christian Doctrine* 3.16.
2. Augustine, *Homilies on John* 26.1.
3. Bernard, *The Love of God* 4.11.

Chapter 3

1. As is pointed out by T.W. Manson in *The Teaching*, p.308.

Chapter 4

1. *Mekhilta* (rabbinical commentary) on Exodus 31:14.

Chapter 8

1. R. Bultmann, *The History of the Synoptic Tradition* (Oxford, 1963), p.138.

2. E.g. by J.N. Farquhar, *The Crown of Hinduism* (Oxford, 1913); cf. E.J. Sharpe, *Not to Destroy but to Fulfil* (Lund, 1965).
3. *The Sayings*, p.135.

Chapter 10

1. E. Brunner, *The Divine Imperative* (London, 1937), p.350.

Chapter 11

1. H. Latimer, Sermon preached in St. Edward's Church, Cambridge, in 1529, quoted in J.P. Smyth, *How We Got Our Bible* (London, [1885] 1938), p.102.

Chapter 13

1. Eusebius, *Ecclesiastical History* 6.8.2.

Chapter 15

1. Théodore de Bèze (Beza) to King Charles IX of France at the Abbey of Poissy, near Paris, in 1561.

Chapter 16

1. A. Whyte, *Lord, Teach Us to Pray*, second edition (London, 1948), pp.33–35.

Chapter 18

1. *The Scofield Reference Bible*, second edition (Oxford,

1917), p.1,002. The sharpness of the antithesis is modified in *The New Scofield Reference Edition* (Oxford, 1967), p.1,000.

Chapter 20

1. *Didache* 9.5.

Chapter 21

1. E. Gosse, *Father and Son* (London, 1928), pp.265–267.
2. Plato, *Republic* 2. 382a–b.

Chapter 22

1. M. Arnold, *Literature and Dogma* (London, 1895), p.95.
2. D.S. Cairns, *The Faith that Rebels* (London, 1928), p.25.
3. *The Sayings*, pp. 89–90.

Chapter 23

1. Tennyson, *In Memoriam*, xxxvi
2. C.F.D. Moule, *The Birth of the New Testament*, third edition (London, 1981), p.117.
3. *The Teaching*, pp. 75–80.

Chapter 24

1. To this source (commonly labelled M) may also be assigned Matthew 18:17, with its direction that the insubordinate brother should be treated 'as a Gentile and a tax collector'.

Chapter 25

1. A. Schweitzer, *The Quest of the Historical Jesus* (London, 1910), p.357.
2. *The Quest*, p.369.
3. T.W. Manson, *Studies in the Gospels and Epistles* (Manchester, 1962), pp.9–10.

Chapter 26

1. S.G.F. Brandon, *Jesus and the Zealots* (Manchester, 1967), p.172.

Chapter 30

1. Justin, *Dialogue with Trypho* 88.3.
2. *Gospel of Thomas*, Saying 82; also in Origen, *Homilies on Jeremiah* 20.3.

Chapter 35

1. *Yalqut Shim'oni* (medieval compilation) 1.766.

Chapter 39

1. T.W. Manson, *The Sayings*, p.87.

Chapter 40

1. *The Sayings*, pp.72–73.
2. D. Hill, *The Gospel of Matthew* (London, 1972), p.162.

Chapter 41

1. *The Sayings*, p.73. Cf. M. Hengel, *The Charismatic Leader and his Followers* (Edinburgh, 1981), pp.1–20: in view of the urgent nearness of the kingdom of God there is no time to lose; all ordinary human considerations and ties must give way to this.
2. A. Gammie, *Rev. John McNeill: his Life and Work* (Glasgow, 1939), p.201.

Chapter 44

1. *Shir ha-Shirim Rabba* 5:2.

Chapter 46

1. Bunyan, *The Pilgrim's Progress,* Part 2.

Chapter 48

1. B.M. Metzger, *A Textual Commentary on the Greek New Testament* (London/New York, 1971), p.169.
2. H.B. Swete, *The Gospel according to St. Mark,* third edition (London, 1909), p.229.
3. Babylonian Talmud, tractate *Berakot* 55 b.

Chapter 51

1. C.S. Lewis, *The Problem of Pain* (London, 1940), p.115.
2. J. Denney, *The Way Everlasting* (London, 1911), p.171. It is noteworthy that, in the judgment of all the nations, it is similarly failure to care for those in need that incurs the sentence: 'Depart ... into the eternal fire prepared for the devil and his angels' (Matt. 25:41).

Chapter 52

1. *The Sayings*, p.308.

Chapter 53

1. Shakespeare, *The Merchant of Venice*, IV, i.
2. *The Sayings*, p.220.

Chapter 54

1. E. Schweizer, *The Good News According to Mark* (London, 1971), p.215.

Chapter 55

1. Plato, *Phaedo* 69 c.
2. Origen, *Against Celsus* 8.16.
3. *Westminster Shorter Catechism*, Answer to Question 31.
4. Burns, *Holy Willie's Prayer*, stanza 1.
5. J.E. Powell, 'Quicunque Vult', in *Sermons from Great St. Mary's*, ed. H.W. Montefiore (London, 1968), p.96.
6. J. Calvin, *Romans and Thessalonians*, English translation (Edinburgh, 1961), pp.114–115.

Chapter 57

1. Reprinted in W.M. Christie, *Palestine Calling* (London, 1939), pp.118–120.

Chapter 58

1. W. Manson, *Jesus the Messiah* (London, 1943), pp. 29f., 39f.

Chapter 62

1. Palestinian Talmud, tractate *Berakot*, 9.7.
2. T.W. Manson, 'The Cleansing of the Temple', *Bulletin of the John Rylands Library* 33 (1950-51), p.279, n. 1. (He, however, accepted the setting of Luke 13:35 as original and supposed that Jesus was bidding temporary farewell to the people of Galilee, saying that they would next see him in Jerusalem.)

Chapter 63

1. *Synoptic Tradition*, p.125.
2. Cf. G.H. Lang, *The Revelation of Jesus Christ* (London, 1945), pp.70, 387.

Chapter 64

1. *The Sayings*, p.147.

Chapter 67

1. Josephus, *Jewish War* 2.125.
2. T.W. Manson, *Ethics and the Gospel* (London, 1960), p.90.
3. *The Sayings*, p.341.

Chapter 68

1. Cf. A. Deissmann, *Light from the Ancient East,* second edition (London, 1927), pp. 125-131.

Chapter 70

1. J. Denney, *The Death of Christ*, sixth edition (London, 1907), p. 160.

INDEX OF BIBLICAL REFERENCES

INDEX OF AUTHORS, ETC.

NORMAN ANDERSON

THE TEACHING OF JESUS

The second book in the new Jesus Library. **Foreword by Michael Green.**

The teaching of Jesus stands on an Everest alone. No other teaching has had the same impact and influence, in countless lives, in diverse cultures and ages. No other teaching has provoked so much change, or stirred so much debate.

Sir Norman presents Jesus' teaching around the central theme of the Kingdom of God. After an introductory chapter on the authenticity of the Gospels, the book falls into three sections: *the summons to the Kingdom,* including the invitation to 'salvation' and 'eternal life'; *the ethics of the Kingdom*, for the individual, the Church and society; and finally *the consummation of the Kingdom,* including the Holy Spirit, the mission of the Church, and the Second Coming.

PROFESSOR SIR NORMAN ANDERSON OBE was Director of the Institute of Advanced Legal Studies in London. He lives in Cambridge and is the author of *The Mystery of the Incarnation.*

JOHN STOTT

I BELIEVE IN PREACHING

A stirring and persuasive celebration of biblical preaching.
Preface by Canon Michael Green.

Is preaching outmoded? In the television age, with an educated congregation, what relevance can there be in sermons? Often preaching is sleepy, insubstantial, or fails to relate biblical truth to the everyday lives of contemporary Christians. In this context, John Stott's magnificent new study makes vital reading, as one of the greatest modern preachers demonstrates the validity, methods and appropriate content of this uniquely dynamic form of communication. 'Preaching is indispensable to Christianity,' he argues. 'Without preaching a necessary part of its authenticity has been lost.'

JOHN STOTT is Rector Emeritus of All Souls Church, Langham Place, London and Director of the London Institute for Contemporary Christianity.

STEPHEN H. TRAVIS

I BELIEVE IN THE SECOND COMING OF JESUS

A revealing study of the Bible's teaching on the last days.
Preface by Canon Michael Green.

'The courage, the clarity and the teaching skills of Dr Travis in this important book are going to help a great many people. Those who have ceased to believe in the return of Christ will be made to think again. Those who will think of little else may have broader perspectives brought to their attention.'
Michael Green, in his preface.

DR STEPHEN H. TRAVIS is director of academic studies at St John's College, Nottingham.

MICHAEL GREEN

I BELIEVE IN SATAN'S DOWNFALL

'Satan worship, fascination with the occult, black magic, astrology and horoscopes, seances and tarot cards have become the rage. Ouija boards and levitation are to be found in many schools. Despite our professed sophistication, there is today in the West a greater interest in and practice of magic than for three centuries,' writes Michael Green.

'At the same time mankind seems to be gripped by forces far greater than the individual, national or international community can cope with. Never has man's technical competence been greater, yet never has there been a greater threat to the future of *homo sapiens* on earth than there is today.

'This book arose out of these factors, and out of personal experience of dark forces which I had not been trained to expect, but which I have in recent years seen both ravaging lives and being triumphantly routed by the power of the living Christ. I am more than ever confident that Christ won the supreme victory over evil in every shape and form, and that the culmination of all history will demonstrate that fact.'

CANON MICHAEL GREEN is Rector of St Aldates, Oxford.